World Class Contract Management

The ULTIMATE Guide for Purchasing Professionals

Omid Ghamami, MBA

Author - Educator
Consultant - Speaker - Trainer

World Class Contract Management

The ULTIMATE Guide for Purchasing Professionals

By Omid Ghamami, MBA

World Class Contract Management

The ULTIMATE Guide for Purchasing Professionals

Acknowledgements

I'd like to thank Ralph Gillespie, who believed in me and had me start doing negotiation planning, negotiation strategy, total cost analysis, and contract law training for his entire global procurement organization at Intel Corp – which was full of 20 and 30 year purchasing industry veterans - and also had me reviewing all corporate negotiation plans on his behalf - all while I was only 24 years old and not too far removed from graduate school. He saw how much personal research I was doing on negotiation best practices and contract law, and how I was applying it to my areas of responsibility for best in department results. He saw something in me and gave me the keys to the car for his Fortune 50 global purchasing organization, and I've been training purchasing professionals how to be their best ever since. He helped me find my passion and I'm highly indebted to him for putting me on that track to success.

I'd also like to thank Dr. Stu Van Horn, who gave me a gold badge to design and implement the only purchasing curriculum and certificate program in the entire California Community College system. He too believed in me and my cause, and that program is now thriving and looking to be replicated in other higher education institutions. It is one of my proudest accomplishments, but it would have never happened without Dr. Van Horn's efforts to pave the approval path all the way through the system – a process that took five years, but was well worth it in the end.

I'd also like to thank Michelle Stamnes, a highly competent corporate attorney and long time friend. She has always been a great sounding board for me, and has helped me on my journey to embrace contract law and purchasing contracts as a critical enabler of performance and results in purchasing organizations, which ultimately was my motivation behind writing this book.

Finally, I'd like to thank my dad. He taught me – with his actions and not with his words – how to do every business venture first class or not at all, and he taught me the value of integrity, honesty, and commitment in all facets of life. He was also my first negotiations teacher. He taught me how to solve conflict using diplomacy – and he was after all, a former diplomat. He gave me the foundation and the confidence to do all that I do today. This book is ultimately dedicated to him.

Table of Contents

Preface……………………………………………………...…7

Chapter I: Contract Fundamentals………………….......15

Chapter II: Contract Management Importance……...…29

Chapter III: Making the Contract Fit the Purchase……...57

Chapter IV: Analyzing Common Terms & Conditions.....81

Chapter V: Post Contract Management……………...……197

Chapter VI: Final Thoughts……………………………...…221

World Class Contract Management
The Ultimate Reference Guide for Purchasing Professionals

Preface: The purpose of this book and the target audience

This book is intended to give an overview of the highly critical skill of purchasing contract management (or what sales professionals would call 'sales contract management'). It is my experience that purchasing professionals are consistently plagued by inadequate knowledge of purchasing contract law, which becomes a capability and therefore a career liability. The goal of this book is to address this problem and turn this liability to an area of strength and competitive advantage for purchasing professionals.

Although not indicated in the cover page or book title, this book would be of equal value to sales professionals as well. A contract of course is a tool which both parties must know, understand, and utilize to their best advantage. Every sales organization has their own sales contract templates, and the information contained herein is every bit as applicable to the sales side of any business.

This book is not meant to be read once and then put aside, as one might do with a novel. It is meant to be read in its entirety, with certain sections then referenced on an ongoing basis as the need arises, continuously over time. It is intended to be a timeless reference guide, and is written, as so few purchasing books are, not for the academic researcher, but for the practitioner – the person who wants concrete and actionable direction to do their job better and get their career on the fast track.

Because of the prevalence of contracts in our daily lives, it is my belief, conviction, and personal experience that these tools can be applied in any facet of one's personal life as well.

While there is much information in this book, it must all be taken in context, and should be validated internally with the appropriate business partners before being put to use. The author is not an attorney and does not practice law. The legal information contained herein is not meant to substitute the necessary legal reviews needed in negotiating a contract with a supplier. Contents of this book may not be appropriate for all situations. Readers must understand that management and legal direction from within their company should take precedence in every case where conflict is present with information in this book. Although the information contained herein is believed to be accurate, complete, and current, there is no warranty of such, express or implied. It is the responsibility of the reader to verify any information in this book before acting on it. The author and Purchasing Advantage are not liable for how these principles are used in any way whatsoever. The direction in this book is not appropriate for all situations, and may be counterproductive in some. The reader needs to exercise judgment, make sound decisions, and be fully accountable for the outcome.

The writing style of this book is such that it varies from referring to purchasing in third person, as "the purchasing professional," to referring to purchasing in the second person, as "you" or "your." This is deliberate, and the second person is used generally when the guidance is more prescriptive and situation specific.

My passion for writing this book is to bring to life what is one of the most dynamic, fulfilling, and high impact positions within a corporation. The book is written from the vantage point of those who work in mid to large size corporations, with the assumption that there are supporting finance, legal, accounts payable, and other support organizations to work with. For those who work in smaller companies, references to other such functions may have to be interpreted as activities which are fulfilled by purchasing professionals themselves, and if taken in that context, the guidance in this book should still be valuable in that capacity.

My challenge to you: Use the tools here to go forward and make a difference in your firms. Find your purchasing advantage!

Visit Purchasing Advantage Corporate Training and Consulting Services at www.PurchasingAdvantage.com

Chapter I: Contract Fundamentals

The role of the contract in purchasing is critical. Too often, purchasing professionals are not sufficiently versed in purchasing contract law, and as a consequence, rely excessively on their legal department and engage in behaviors that result in lost leverage and total cost opportunities in negotiations.

The most fundamental step in contract management is simply understanding what a contract is. A contract is a vehicle that captures the agreement between parties and also allocates risk. The term 'risk' for purchasing professionals means that there are total cost implications. When a contract states that a supplier is to be indemnified for intellectual property claims on direct material components they are selling to you, the risk has been contractually shifted to you, and this may well have massive total cost implications. There are a myriad of such examples in every contract – some with small implications, others with large implications.

The core components of a contract are offer, acceptance, and consideration. An offer is a promise or commitment that is communicated to the other party using words or conduct that indicates intent to contract. Acceptance entails words or conduct that indicate assent to the offer (i.e. intent to be legally bound), as well as communication to the other party of such. Consideration is something of value for *both* parties (bilateral value), which is what the parties bargain for, representing an exchange of value. This may also include promises, such as a promise not to sue as a form of consideration.

There are different formats in which a contract can take place. Generally speaking, oral is the least desired format, as there is no documentation to capture the agreement in place. Offer, acceptance, and consideration can all be agreed upon orally, but the time savings associated with establishing an oral agreement will often be far superseded by the amount of additional time required to interpret and execute the agreement, as well as time spent trying to manage conflict regarding issues which were not ever well defined or mutually understood.

The next form a contract can take is written. The mistake that many purchasing professionals make is that they attempt to write the contract in "legalese," thinking this is necessary to make the contract official or binding. The contract only needs to capture the entire agreement in a way that is very clear, very understandable, and not subject to interpretation. Using "legalese" is not a requirement for a written contract. There are different types of written agreements, which we will cover later.

Your behavior can also create or modify a contract! Consider a situation whereby a supplier sends a quotation with a set of terms and a signature line to a buyer in a company. The buyer does not respond with counter signature, but instead starts sending delivery dates and order quantities to the supplier. The buyer's behavior has indicated agreement to the contract and its terms. The buyer's behavior will likely be interpreted in the courts as having in fact created a binding contract between the parties. Purchasing professionals need to be having this conversation with all their end users, because they in all likelihood are completely unaware that they can create unintentional contracts with their behavior.

As aforementioned, your behavior can also modify an existing contract. For instance, take the example of a contract that indicates that the payment terms are net 30, but your firm always pays the supplier in 60 days, with the supplier never raising an issue or indicating exception to such contract breach. Let us further say that years later, the supplier now has issue with late payments and takes your company to court to enforce the contract. The courts may likely rule in favor of your firm and determine that the *course of past conduct* has in fact modified the contract to be net 60, despite what the actual language states.

Later in this book, we will cover contract language and ways in which to manage business practices such that the possibility of behavioral modification of contracts is minimized.

Contracts can arise through the signing of what seems like innocent documentation. For instance, many purchasing professionals, and sales professionals as well for that matter, believe that Letters Of Intent (LOI) and Memorandums Of Understanding (MOU) are harmless and non-binding documents. In fact, both of these documents can and usually do contain all three major components of a contract - offer, acceptance, and consideration. Further, such documents rarely carry any of the other more beneficial terms contained in both short and long form contracts, and so they can bring about highly undesirable consequences. It is for these reasons that many firms have a hard and fast policy of not signing LOIs or

MOUs, except under certain circumstances (e.g., executive to executive agreement across companies; LOI or MOU written so carefully that even if considered a contract, it carries very little burden of risk, based on how it was written).

Another example of an unintended contract can take place with the Request for Quote (RFQ) or Request for Proposal (RFP) processes engaged in by purchasing professionals with potential suppliers. These document types shall be collectively referred to as 'RFX' moving forward, with the 'X' denoting that corresponding context applies to both RFP and RFQs. All RFX documentation sent to prospective suppliers should have a visible disclaimer that states "this is not an offer, but rather a solicitation for an offer." Absent this language, the receiving supplier may be able to view the language contained therein as a legal offer and seek to consummate the agreement by defining consideration and accepting. Although this is not commonplace and may not pass the reasonable person test, the goal is to not leave the opportunity for such excursions. The desired situation is for the supplier to make an offer and the buyer to hold the decision to accept or not.

Another key concept to understand is related to who can actually bind a firm to contracts. From the supplier's perspective, any person from a potential or existing client company that approaches them with desire or intent to purchase has authority to do so. The courts generally uphold this perspective, subject once again to the reasonable person test. A supplier can for instance reasonably conclude that an engineer in charge of a key project has authority to bind the company, if the engineer presents themselves in such a fashion. However, a supplier cannot, at least in the eyes of the courts, reasonably conclude that the janitor would have actually authority to bind the company to an engineering contract. This would not pass the court's reasonable person test. It can be said then that there are two types of authority to bind a contract: real authority and apparent authority.

Real authority is when the person who is intending on binding the company to a purchasing contract is in fact internally authorized to do so. This is usually a function of job title and certain internal approval parameters that must have been met. The most common examples include corporate vice presidents, purchasing personnel, and those employees holding corporate procurement cards. In the case of purchasing personnel, they are inherently authorized to bind the firm to agreements, subject to certain restrictions and pre-approval requirements. These restrictions may be related to a maximum contract value, as well as approval from management and/or legal and/or finance and/or the internal customer. There can therefore be a situation whereby purchasing personnel do not in fact have real authority to negotiate an agreement. This is not the supplier's job to determine or even ask, and the courts will generally support this position.

Once again, the courts will likely apply the reasonable person test and determine if the supplier acted reasonably by believing the purchasing professional had authority to engage in contract negotiations and bind their company. Corporate vice presidents are those that generally have been appointed by the board of directors, or are otherwise authorized to bind the firm to contractual agreements with external third parties. This is as opposed to appointed vice presidents, who typically are not authorized to do so. This very much depends on corporate structure however. For instance, the reason banks have so many vice presidents is so that they have many people who are able to sign the vast amount of contractual agreements that banks face on a regular and routine basis.

With apparent authority, this can really include almost anyone in a firm, subject to the reasonable person test. Even a secretary may be able to present themselves as having authority to commit a firm to an agreement, with the supplier acting reasonably by accepting the secretary as having authority to do so. Of course it depends on the situation. If the secretary is trying to negotiate for the acquisition of another company, it is not in any way reasonable for the other party to accept that this secretary has the authority to engage in committing the firm to such a transaction. However, if the secretary is working with a hotel and with caterers to book a corporate event, it is entirely reasonable for those suppliers to assume that the secretary has authority to engage in such negotiations.

Apparent authority is then anyone within a company who has the ability to reasonably present themselves as having authority to bind the firm. When taken at that definition, it can actually almost include anyone in the firm under the right circumstances, and once again, the courts do not generally view it as the supplier's job to research and validate whether someone who presents themselves as having authority actually does, unless they are being blatantly unreasonable in doing so.

Given the above, the risk of undesired, suboptimal, and poorly reached agreements by unauthorized individuals acting under apparent authority are an everyday risk that purchasing departments face. Interestingly, employees that grant themselves apparent authority and create liability for a firm, with no internal approvals or willfully against corporate policies, may be found personally liable for corresponding damages that come about as a result. Internal customers must therefore be educated by the purchasing department to understand the difference between real and apparent authority and both the corporate and personal risks that may be incurred when unauthorized, suboptimal, or unintended purchasing transactions take place.

The basis for purchasing contract law is twofold. The first component is based on Uniform Commercial Code Article 2 (hereafter, 'UCC'). UCC applies to the purchase of goods only, and has been adopted by all states in near uniform fashion with the exception of the state of Louisiana, which has their own customized version that they use. The state laws under which a contract is governed will be covered later in this book. The second component is common law, which applies to the sale of services. Common law has been developed based on past court decisions and precedents set by judges, rather than through legislation. Therefore, a historical legal metric is used to ensure consistency with past decisions and rulings.

There is a third type of governing law that is seen less frequently, but is getting some visibility. This is CISG, or Convention on the International Sale of Goods. This may take place of UCC in contracts where it is specified that this is the case. As of the time of this writing, UCC is the far more common precedent in domestic (United States) contracts for goods, even when contracting with foreign suppliers.

When forming a contract for the purchase of goods, there may be many aspects of the agreement which are not addressed, for a variety of reasons, ranging from oversight to practicality to planned omission. In the case of contracts for the sale of goods, UCC "gap fillers" are said to apply, giving legal coverage to those areas where nothing was addressed by either party in the agreement but coverage applies from UCC. The good news is that these gap fillers often favor the purchasing professional, but once again, it is always better to take the route of documented contract clarity, versus the potentially time consuming and unpredictable route of relying on assumptions and gap fillers. For common law, gap fillers do not apply, and agreement is required on all the material terms.

Chapter II: Contract Management Importance

Contract management is something done by both purchasing and sales professionals.   It is also done by legal personnel in corporations as well.   Contract management entails ensuring the right types of contracts are in place with the right suppliers, in such a way that Total Cost of Ownership (hereafter, TCO) is minimized, agility over the life of the contract is maximized, and legal risk levels are optimized.   These can be considered the three legs to the contract management stool, and all three need to be in place and functioning for the stool to be usable.

The life cycle of a contract does not end once it is signed – though many purchasing professionals claim victory at this moment and quickly move onto the next contract negotiation. In fact, much of the heavy lifting begins *after* the contract is signed. Forming a contract is a "pay now or pay later" activity; the less attention paid to detail, content, and completeness while forming the contract, the more work will be waiting for the purchasing professional post contract signature in the form of contract excursions and ambiguity management. This relationship is also disproportional, as "paying later" is usually much more costly than exercising due diligence up front.

Proper contract management involves a number of things: establishment of contracts (short and long forms), contracting with the right suppliers, mitigating risk, minimizing TCO, preventing excursions, managing excursions, keeping the company legal, and encouraging supplier continuous quality and performance improvement. We will explore each of these now.

The desire to minimize TCO is well documented and understood amongst the purchasing community. It is not always practiced well though. A purchasing professional can purchase something at a very low acquisition price, yet create a huge total cost liability for their organization in doing so. This example applies well to cars; a high mileage twenty year old

Yugo brand automobile can be acquired very cheap – maybe for $100 or less. However, TCO will be a different equation entirely, and it is highly likely in this instance that the maintenance bill just on the drive home will exceed what was paid for the car.

Contract management is no different. Take the example of a raw material component that is purchased with intent to embed in a product that will be then sold to consumers and retailers. If the contract stipulates that patents are pending but not finalized or approved, and no indemnification protection is provided in the contract, the purchasing professional's organization can be subsequently exposed to massive patent infringement lawsuits. While this example may not be representative, it certainly is not the exception either.

There are a myriad of errors, omissions, and oversights that can have significant TCO impacts to almost any sort of purchase transaction. For instance, a Fortune 50 company was ordering capital equipment for their product manufacturing lines. While in ground transport to the company, the truck was involved in an accident, and the equipment was damaged and needed replacement. The contract stipulated that the equipment was to be replaced at the supplier's expense, but did not stipulate in what time frame, and the damages were limited to the value of the contract. Because that manufacturing line could not run absent this equipment, millions of dollars of lost revenue and profits ensued, as the supplier took weeks to provide another working unit to this company's specifications – all the while being in complete compliance to the buyer's contract.

The above is just one of many, many examples where a contract can dramatically impact the TCO of a purchase transaction. What may seem like a great deal at the time of signing may in fact be a huge TCO fiasco, which may not only be devastating to the buyer's firm, but also to the buyer's career.

Agility is another critical concept. Businesses need to move fast, purchasing professionals have many contracts to negotiate, and internal customers will always have pressing deadlines they have to meet. The ability to engage in agile negotiations is critical. However, the need for agility does not end there.

The contract itself needs to enable business agility for as long as it is in effect. Both of those factors (contract negotiation agility, and the subsequent enablement of business agility by the contract) are directly owned by purchasing. Improper and suboptimal purchasing practices as it relates to contract management, to be covered later in this book, will dramatically increase the cycle time and overall results of negotiations. Furthermore, contracts that do not aid in prevention and remedy of undesired situations will become an impediment rather than an enabler to the organization.

There are many self defeating behaviors and practices by purchasing professionals that make the contract more of a liability than a benefit. All of these will be introduced in this section, but will covered in more detail in later chapters.

The first self defeating contract management practice on the part of purchasing professionals is using a purchase order, which usually carries fewer and less encompassing terms, as the contract for what really requires a long for contract for reasons of contract value, risk, or criticality.

Another common self defeating contract practice is simply attaching the supplier quotation to the buyer's standard contract template and believing that the contract is complete. This causes problems for a variety of reasons. One is that there will in all likelihood be conflicting terms between the quotation (where the supplier often embeds terms) and the buyer's standard contract template. Another issue is that the contract will not have been customized in any way to the purchase, and therefore will not likely offer adequate protection (recall the capital equipment that got damaged in a truck shipment accident). Finally, the end result at best will be a contract for resources (goods and/or services) instead of a contract for supplier performance results.

The next self defeating behavior that purchasing professionals often engage in is developing and using the contract as a seat belt in the case of an accident instead of as a powerful vehicle to enable and ensure high quality supplier performance. What is often times viewed as a bad supplier is in all actuality just a bad contract design.

The next common way in which purchasing professionals engage in self defeating contract management behavior is by allowing the legal department to own the contract instead of taking personal accountability. Then when the legal department approves the contract there is often the incorrect perception that the legal department has endorsed this as a good contract and therefore it is. The legal department is only looking at legal risks and exposures. The contract may be acceptable – or even outstanding - in that regards, but it may still in fact be a terrible contract for the business.

The final self defeating behavior that purchasing professionals often engage in is allowing the supplier to redline the contract. Related to this is the practice of saving the Ts and Cs for last in negotiations, which fully encourages the supplier to markup the contract. As with all the self defeating contract management behaviors noted, this should never be allowed to happen in the first place.

Moving back to the third key focus area of contract management, legal risk optimization is also critical. Most of you may wonder why the desire is not to minimize legal risk. The reason is that without legal risk, the business cannot operate. There is always the risk of getting sued by a supplier, for instance. The best way to avoid this with 100% certainty is to never sign any contracts at all. Obviously this is impossibility. Similarly, insurance level requirements for suppliers could be raised to five times higher than normal for maximum risk reduction. However, this will without a doubt result in a commensurate price increase to the purchasing professional. So we can say that the goal is not to minimize legal risk, but rather to optimize it. Optimizing legal risk entails getting the maximum benefit for the minimum amount of legal risk.

There are different levels of risk, and those need to be understood, with determinations made as to what the tradeoff is (risk vs results), and decisions made from there. There are two primary factors to look at when making legal risk decisions: one is the impact of the risk being undertaken and the other is the probability of such risk manifesting itself. These must then be contrasted with what the expected or potential benefit is of taking this risk. This risk model can be viewed in matrix format, in which darker shading indicates higher overall risk, which must be offset by higher overall business returns.

Low	High	Highest
Low	Medium	High
Lowest	Low	Medium

Probability of Risk

Impact of Risk

This overall matrix shall be referred to as depicting 'compound risk', as this is a measure of risk subject to both the impact and the probability of such risk, and as such is a compounded definition of risk. There is no mathematical formula for either impact or probability of risk that is readily available for most legal risk situations. In other words, determining exactly which cell in the matrix your particular contract management circumstance falls into is a largely subjective decision, but with the input of other stakeholders (internal customer, legal), this decision can be made with more confidence and authority. Business decisions then need to be made in terms of what the tradeoff is between this level of compound risk and the amount of business benefit. There are few circumstances where it makes sense to enter into a legal risk situation that is characterized as 'high' in the compound risk matrix, but exceptions can be found.

For instance, a manufacturing firm had 20% capacity growth requirements and needed to build new plants and purchase new equipment to accommodate, which represented a major expense – over ten million dollars of investment were needed. However, they found a small supplier out of Israel that had developed a software application that would increase the throughput rate of just one piece of manufacturing equipment in the manufacturing lines. This piece of equipment was the bottleneck of the existing manufacturing lines, and this software improved this equipment's production rate by 22%, providing the same benefit for the entire manufacturing line.

So why was this significant? Well, this meant that the existing manufacturing equipment could be improved to handle the increased capacity instead of building new plants, buying new equipment and hiring new employees. The business benefit was beyond question; this increased capacity could be handled for a fraction of the cost of obtaining new property, plant, and equipment.

However, the compound risk in this scenario was formidable. The supplier was small, came from a volatile region, was extremely revenue thirsty, and their brain trust was comprised of just a few individuals – any of whom could quit, get called off to compulsory military requirement, win the lottery, or even drop dead of a heart attack. There was no backup plan for these people. In addition, they were difficult to work with. They often promised new or desired features and did not deliver, and were always begging for early progress payments and for funds to be received before the end of each fiscal quarter, to make their books look good.

The probability of an excursion – any kind of excursion – with this supplier was both of high impact and probability. However, the product was tested on a prototype manufacturing line, and it did indeed deliver the 22% throughput rate improvement that was promised. The business decision was made to accept the compound risk, because the business return was so high. Additionally, the compound risk was reduced through the addition of a contract clause that introduced an escrow account to always house the latest version of the software object and source code, such that if the supplier did go out of business, the customer could still have legal rights and access to the software and pursue another company to manage software program maintenance. The decision was made to proceed and it was the right decision for the business – legal risks and all.

We have already established that firms look to manage risks through the establishment of contracts. Well written contracts define which parties bear the burden of which risks, under which circumstances, and to what extent. Poorly written contracts don't do any of these things well, and often result in "fire drills," as both parties try to determine how to remedy an issue or excursion, given the contract gives unclear direction or worse yet, none at all. There are many different types of contracts, but for now, we will classify them as two different types: short and long form.

Short form contracts are those that are sent out with a purchase order. Long form agreements are those that generally are greater in length, complexity, specificity, coverage, protection, and customization to what is being ordered, and require a signature by authorized representatives of both parties. Short form contracts are not negotiated per se, they are just sent with the purchase order to the supplier, through whatever means of transmission is used. Long form agreements typically require customization and negotiation, both of which may become very time consuming activities. For many transactions, the nature of the risk, criticality of purchase, or amount being spent are such that long form contracts are required.

The obvious question is "why not use a long form for all purchases?" The answer has to do with optimization of time and risk. Most large companies have thousands of suppliers, over 90% of which only receive one purchase order a year. These purchases are often low risk, low dollars, low criticality, or some combination thereof. It is not worth the time and energy to put long form contracts in place.

Further, putting long form contracts in place with all suppliers signifies that all suppliers are a critical part of the organization's supplier base, when in fact the opposite is usually true; undesired growth of the supplier base is a major problem for most large companies.

Undesired supply base growth happens as a consequence of the general employee base engaging in end user driven purchasing decisions, resulting in new supplier additions that may be good for the employee and their particular need, but bad for the company in the aggregate. Because there are too many of these situations for purchasing to individually address, and assuming the case of a low expenditure/low risk/low criticality purchase, purchasing will usually simply issue a purchase order, and have it go out with the short form contract forming the basis for the agreement.

Typically, a larger company will have 5% or less of their total supplier base under long form contract, but 80 – 90% of their total expenditures under long form contract. The key is to make sure the right subset of the supplier base is under long form contract and the majority of the company's dollars are being managed well.

The following checklist will aid in determination of what type of contract to use. If the answer to any of these questions is "yes," then a long form contract should be considered:

- Is there a high contract value (this figure will be very company specific and should encompass aggregated forecast spends, not just a singular transaction that may be required now)?
- Are there any intellectual property considerations involved?
- Is there any custom or developmental software being purchased?
- Is this considered a strategic supplier (e.g. direct materials provider, technology partner, etc)?
- Are the goods being purchased high risk (e.g. toxic chemicals, manufacturing equipment, critical raw materials)?
- Will there be on site services, construction work, or complex or recurring service arrangements?

If it is decided based on the above or based on other factors that a long form contract will be used, the decision making process is not done. The purchasing professional then needs to decide what type of long form contract will be used. While there are a large number of situation and industry specific contract templates, the focus here will be on the most common ones: goods, services, and goods and services. All of these should be available through the legal department of most medium to large sized companies. It is important that the latest version is obtained rather than using a dated one saved on one's hard drive. Contract templates are living documents that are always being updated to provide the most complete protection and coverage and to reflect the latest changes in the business and legal environment.

Goods long form agreements have terms and conditions (Ts and Cs) that are specific to the purchase of goods absent any services component. The purchasing professional must pay careful attention when using this template, because often times the goods being purchased also come with a service component as well – installation, consulting, training, maintenance, etc. If it is deemed that no service components are involved and the purchase is also not for construction or software, then the goods long form agreement is likely the best one for this arrangement.

Services long form agreements have Ts and Cs that are specific to the purchase of services absent any goods components. Once again, the purchasing professional must be careful when using this template. Take the example of a janitorial service, for instance. If the supplier is also providing chemicals and providing and stocking toilet paper and paper towels, then a services long form agreement may not be sufficient to cover all aspects of the agreement, and a goods and services long form template may be more appropriate. However, if it is found that no goods are being purchased whatsoever, then the services long form is likely the right agreement template. The major exception is where the services are towards the development of intellectual property, in which case an intellectual property contract probably needs to be drafted, with heavy involvement by the legal department. As a rule of thumb, it is always a good idea to get the legal department involved up front when there is intellectual property development involved.

Goods and services agreements are used for instances as outlined above, where both goods and services are being procured. They do not need to be purchased in equal dollar quantities or in a certain amount, they just need to both be purchased as a part of the agreement. This will provide for clauses that cover both such purchases.

There are still other types of contracts which are used far less often, and therefore are of lesser focus in this book. These include construction contracts, software contracts, and intellectual property (IP) agreements.

The most important thing to remember when developing a contract is that the standard contract template doesn't "know" what it is that you are actually purchasing. The contract template was, by design, written to be generic and applicable to just about any situation that would merit use of that contract template. Therefore, there will be clauses that are inappropriate, inapplicable, not specific enough, or offer too much detail for what is being purchased.

As stated earlier, far too many purchasing professionals simply affix a supplier's quotation to a long form contract as an addendum and think that they have performed the necessary legal diligence to protect their company's interests. In fact time and energy needs to be devoted to modifications, additions, and customizations of the contract, in the form of amendments and addendums. This is all a part of the "pay now or pay later" nature of contract management.

It is the purchasing department's job to contract with companies that are in the best interest of their employer, not necessarily those that are in the perceived best interest of the internal customer. While the internal customer might want to use a certain supplier with whom they have familiarity and experience, this may be in conflict with a more comprehensive corporate strategy that the purchasing professional is pursuing that does not involve this supplier.

Customer service does not mean making the internal customer delighted; it means enabling them to meet their business requirements in a way that is consistent with what the board of directors, internal audit, and the stockholders (as applicable) would find to be in the best interests of the company. These then are the companies that purchasing professionals should seek to put under contract.

As aforementioned, usually only 5% or less of the total supply base is considered strategic and is worthy of establishing long form contracts with, although this figure will be much different in a purely capital equipment or direct materials environment, where this figure may reach closer to 80% of a much smaller supply base. Aside from contracting with the right suppliers, other objectives purchasing should pursue when developing contracts are mitigating risk, minimizing TCO, preventing excursions, managing excursions, encouraging and enabling supplier performance, and keeping the company legal.

Another purpose of contract management, largely accomplished in the contract formulation stage, is establishment of contract language that aids in the prevention of excursions. An excursion can be defined as anything that happens in the course of business with the supplier that is undesired, such as excursions related to safety, quality, delivery, payment, pricing, performance, maintenance, customer service, or the overall supply line.

It is generally true that those purchasing managers that are very good at "putting out fires" (i.e., managing excursions that arise) are well recognized for being savvy problem solvers, meanwhile, those that never allow fires to start in the first place tend to go unnoticed in this regards. Ultimately though, the purchasing professional that doesn't allow the excursions to happen in the first place is better able to allocate their time to more value added activities, and therefore generates better overall results and enjoys a better career progression.

In order to ensure that the proper language is in place to minimize the probability of excursions, the purchasing professional must do a thorough preventative assessment with the internal customer. The customer must be asked "what are all the things that may go wrong after we sign the agreement?" The customer should be given the sample categories provided above, ranging from safety to supply line. Every single probable scenario should be laid and out and defined by the customer.

The purchasing professional should ask probing questions to fuel the dialogue and ensure completeness of customer thought process. The purchasing professional should then augment these with his or her own concerns. Then for all of these, measures need to be put in the contract that address both expectations and remedies.

Let's go back to the example of manufacturing equipment, which is an ideal example to work with, as this is one of those "no excursions accepted" type of contracts, because manufacturing downtime equates to lost profits. Prior to contracting for the business, purchasing works with the internal customer, a manufacturing engineer, to capture any and all concerns that the customer may have regarding the purchase. Note that these concerns have to be focused not just on the purchase transaction, but also (and more importantly) everything that can go wrong after the product is already acquired.

It is not enough, however, for purchasing to simply capture the customer's concerns. There must be an understanding of how these concerns or issues, if manifested, may impact the business. Further, it must be understood how to both prevent and respond to such concerns and issues, the latter being important in cases such incidents cannot be prevented or in fact are not prevented. The absolute emphasis must be on how to prevent excursions. Remember, the value in a contract lies not in its ability to be a great safety net after excursions, but rather, its ability to guide the supplier such that excursions never take place to begin with.

A systemic approach is needed to manage this process and to ensure that every major risk has contract measures in place from both a preventative and a responsive perspective. This analytical process has been captured in the following fashion for this manufacturing capital equipment example (this template is a recommended approach):

Concern	Business Impact	Preventative Contract Measure	Contract Remedy
Late deliveries of capital equipment	Manufacturing downtime	Late deliveries contractually documented as being a material breach of contract	Contractual price reduction for every day late; consequential damages to cover lost profits
Capital equipment malfunction during production	Manufacturing downtime	Warranty clause defines exact product performance criteria; requirement for supplier to have local access to critical spare parts on demand	Aggressive contractual time frame within which supplier must remedy warranty breach, at their cost; consequential damages to cover lost profits after this period
Capital equipment is irreparably damaged in transit	Manufacturing downtime	FOB supplier dock language to ensure supplier responsibility until final delivery	Requirement that supplier have a spare unit always available within 24 hours of notification of receipt of non-functional unit; consequential damages to cover lost profits after this period
Supplier goes out of business and equipment operating system goes unsupported.	Manufacturing productivity impacts or downtime	Contractual language that places the supplier's source & object code in 3rd party escrow account.	Contractual right to shift this source code and object code to a third party provider to manage and make updates to.

In assessing the areas above, it is highly unlikely and in fact improbable that the standard goods contract of most firms would address both preventative and remedial measures for this particular purchase to the necessary degree desired as outlined here. This gap between ideal contract language (the output of the above exercise) and standard contract language is one of the biggest and most common issues that purchasing professionals face.

The problem lies in the fact that the vast majority of supplier management issues are a function of poorly written contracts. To make matters worse, purchasing professionals often find themselves so busy with supplier management issues that they don't have time to address this front end component of the cycle, thus continuing the cycle. The intent of this section is to educate purchasing professionals on this topic and urge them to break free of this vicious cycle by addressing the root cause instead of constantly addressing the symptoms. The next chapter deals with this concept exclusively.

Chapter III: Making the Contract Fit the Purchase

The previous chapter established the importance that purchasing professionals must place on knowing how, when, and why to make the right changes to the standard contract template. We will now explore the methodology used to make these changes.

It should be noted that the introduction of changes to an agreement is only done with long form contracts. If the purchasing professional finds themselves in a situation where changes to a short form contract are required, then this likely indicates they are using the wrong contract format, and they should be using a long form contract instead.

The fact that short form contracts are typically issued directly by an accounts payable computer system to the supplier in an automated fashion along with the PO makes it even less feasible to modify these terms. Changes to the standard long form contract agreement are done through addendums and amendments. We will explore these two concepts below.

An amendment represents a modification to existing language into the body of a contract, whereas an addendum represents the introduction of new information to an agreement, in appendix fashion. Neither carry more or less legal weight than the other, but rather play different yet equally significant roles. It is important that purchasing professionals know how to use both properly.

An amendment is used when existing language in the body of the contract lacks desired information, contains inapplicable information, lacks desired specificity, or has incorrect information for that specific purchase. An addendum is used when new contract language is being added to the contract, as opposed to modifying what language already exists in it.   This will typically entail a new clause or contract section altogether, whereas amendments typically modify existing clauses. Let us explore both concepts further.

Take the example of a standard payment terms clause in section IX, subsection A of a hypothetical contract that reads as follows:

IX.   Payment and Invoicing

A) Payment shall be made by Buyer to Supplier based on 2/10 Net 45 payment terms. The time period for tracking payment terms shall begin from the time Buyer receives an acceptable invoice from Supplier and shall end at the time of payment transmission by Buyer to Seller.

This short clause tells us many things. The first is that the terms 'Buyer' and 'Seller' are defined somewhere in the contract, likely in the Definitions section of the agreement. We know this because both words are capitalized, despite the fact that they do not meet standard grammatical rules for capitalization (pronoun or the beginning of a sentence). The next thing we know is that the Supplier is willing to extend the Buyer a 2% discount if the Buyer chooses to pay within 10 days. We also know that if that option is not exercised, payment in full from Buyer to Supplier is due in 45 days. Finally, we know that the payment clock starts upon the receipt of an acceptable invoice and ends upon the transmission of payment. It is implied but not stated that the invoice must be acceptable to the Buyer (as opposed to acceptable to the Seller or to both), since the Supplier would have already found it acceptable or they wouldn't have sent it.

Now let us say that the supplier has agreed to a modification of these terms, for a 1/10 Net 60 payment term model. Let us also say that the purchasing professional has agreed to a penalty of 1% for every week which payment is made (note: this is for example only and it is not recommended that purchasing professionals ever agree to a late payment penalty).

The temptation in this example is to simply go in and change the verbiage in this standard contract clause to reflect these changes, however, doing so can be problematic. The reason for this is that contracts need to be easy to pick up by anyone in the purchasing ranks, with the ability to quickly assess what is different in this contract from the standard corporate template. If the terms are simply modified in the body of the contract with no indications of where or how, making this assessment is near impossible, as one would have to tediously compare this contract to the corporate template – something nobody has time for.

There are two acceptable methods to making contract amendments, but in either case, amendments need to be done in the same exact fashion in the entirety of the agreement; flipping back and forth between methods in the same contract is not an acceptable practice. The first method is to make changes in the body of the clause using revisions mode or track changes mode. This will clearly show what language has been stricken and what verbiage has been added. An example of this is shown below.

IX.   Payment and Invoicing

A) Payment shall be made by Buyer to Supplier based on 2~~1~~/10 Net ~~45~~ <u>60</u> payment terms. The time period for tracking payment terms shall begin from the time Buyer receives an acceptable invoice from Supplier and shall end at the time of payment transmission by Buyer to Seller. <u>Should Buyer transmit payment later than the terms noted above, this shall be considered a breach of contract and there shall be a 1% penalty assessed for every week for which said payment is delayed.</u>

As you can see, those items that have been stricken have a line through them and those items that have been added are underlined. This makes it very clear how the standard contract has been modified in this particular section.

The other way in which to introduce amendments is through the addition of a section at the end of the contract which is entitled 'Amendments' and is referenced on the front page of the contract as being one of the components included in the contract between the parties. The example below illustrates how this particular amendment would be captured:

Amendments

A) Section IX, subsection A: In the first sentence beginning with "Payment" and ending with "terms," change the payment terms to be noted as 1/10 Net 60. Additionally, a sentence is to be added to the end of this clause reading as follows: "Should Buyer transmit payment later than the terms noted above, this shall be considered a breach of contract and there shall be a 1% penalty assessed for every week for which said payment is delayed."

Moving onto addendums, these are typically introduced to interject information such as product specifications, service specifications, supplier performance guarantees, and most commonly, supplier quotations for pricing and related terms. These should be done in a separate section at the end of the contract, after the amendments section (if present), and should again also be referenced on the front page of the contract as being one of the components included in the contract between the parties (this language is typically standard in most long form corporate contract templates). This section can include scanned documentation, reference to supplier brochures, detailed scope of work or product specifications, or any other information of relevance to the agreement that does not otherwise belong in a particular contract clause that is already in the contract.

Because the addendum is typically an aggregation of individually unrelated information components (though they are in aggregate related to the contract as a whole), it is recommended to separate by section, such that each set of addendum information is individually identifiable and can also thereby be individually referenced in the body of the agreement where necessary. In such instances, it is recommended to have a cover sheet that simply acts as an addendum separator, and each section thereafter can have its own page or pages, with a section header entitled "Section I – XYZ", "Section II – XYZ", "Section III – XYZ", etc. "XYZ" would then get replaced with whatever it is that is being captured in that particular addendum section, such as "Section I – Supplier Product Pricing", "Section II – Product Performance Specifications", "Section III – Supplier Product Brochure, version 8/3/12", etc. The addendum cover sheet can state in conspicuous font something like what is shown below:

Contract Addendum

Contents:

Section I – Supplier Product Pricing

Section II – Product Performance Specifications

Section III – Supplier Product Brochure, version 8/3/12

Etc.

Now say for instance that the items being purchased have a complex pricing model associated with them, with tiered discounts based on volume and varying discounts based on the actual items being purchased. This is in all likelihood too much information to embed into the pricing clause of the contract. At the same time, it is also not appropriate to ignore that this detailed information exists in the verbiage contained in the pricing clause of the contract. A convenient solution is to reference the Addendum section of the contract in that clause. A simple sentence can be added (as an amendment) to the end of the pricing clause that states "Pricing shall be in accordance with the terms contained in the contract addendum, under Section I – Supplier Product Pricing."

Now that the methodology of doing addendums and amendments are understood, it is important to review more meaningful examples of when they should be used. Say for instance that there is a purchase of servers being made for an information technology data center of a company in the financial services business. Since the data center houses customer critical information, uptime of the data center is of the utmost importance.

Let us say that for this particular purchase, the warranty clause in the standard contract reads as follows (note: this is from a real industry contract):

IX.   Product Warranty

(a) The Seller warrants that the Goods and Services and any part thereof will be of satisfactory quality and free from any defect in manufacture or any defect arising out of design, materials or workmanship, assembly or installation for a period of one (1) year from the date of acceptance of the Goods or Services by the Buyer (hereinafter referred to as "the Warranty Period").

(b) Where during the Warranty Period the Goods or any part or unit thereof is found by the Buyer to be defective, the Seller shall at the written request of the Buyer, replace the same at the risk and expense (including transport costs and other incidental charges) of the Seller or if the Buyer agrees, make good or repair the same at the risk and expense (including transport costs and other incidental charges) of the Seller within 60 days from the date of the written demand from the Buyer to replace, make good or repair the same. The Goods or part or unit so replaced or repaired being then subject to the warranty for a further period of one (1) year from the date of receipt by the Buyer of the Goods or part of unit so replaced or repaired. If the Seller fails to make good or repair the Goods as stated herein, the Buyer reserves the right without prejudice to its other rights under the Contract or otherwise to buy such defective Goods from alternative sources or have the

Goods repaired at alternative sources and all additional costs incurred thereby shall be recoverable from the Seller.

(c) The Seller warrants that it will select and furnish personnel experienced and skilled in the type of work they are to perform under the Contract and that the Services to be performed under the Contract will be performed with due care and diligence and in a workmanlike manner within the turnaround time specified by the Buyer and in accordance with the Buyer's requirements. In the event the Services or part thereof do not conform to the requirements under the Contract, the Seller shall forthwith re-perform the Services. Until such time as the defective Services are re- performed to the satisfaction of the Buyer, the Buyer shall not be obliged to make payment therefore or, if payment has already been made, the Seller shall refund to the Buyer all sums paid.   Any additional or incidental costs related to the re-performance of the Services or part thereof shall be borne solely by the Seller.

This warranty clause seems very robust, but it really depends on what you are purchasing – and remember, the contract has no idea what you are purchasing, it is just a standard template. It is the purchasing professional's job to make it come to life and really be a tool to enable high quality supplier performance. Once again, we are talking about the procurement of servers for a data center for a financial services company. With that in mind, let's break this clause above done, section by section.

Let's look at section (a) of this clause again:

(a) The Seller warrants that the Goods and Services and any part thereof will be of satisfactory quality and free from any defect in manufacture or any defect arising

70

out of design, materials or workmanship, assembly or installation for a period of one (1) year from the date of acceptance of the Goods or Services by the Buyer (hereinafter referred to as "the Warranty Period").

What we know from reading this is that a number of words are pre-defined in the contract. This is usually done in a clause at the beginning of the contract that is called "Definitions". We can also see that there has been a new word defined in this clause ("The Warranty Period") instead of in the "Definitions" clause. This is of some concern, because it means the purchasing professional needs to be on the constant lookout for defined words that could be anywhere in the contract – instead of all in one place.

The next thing we can see in this section of the clause is that the Seller is only warranting that the servers will be of "satisfactory quality". What does this mean? What is the definition of "satisfactory"? Who decides what "satisfactory" means? This is completely unacceptable in a contract of this type. The purchasing professional needs to put performance specification in the contract that the product must adhere to. Simply putting "satisfactory quality" leaves a huge unknown in the contract and also leaves ample room for the supplier to argue that what they provided was in fact satisfactory, or at least satisfactory to them. The only way around this is to make the criteria for quality defined in objective criteria, which absolutely can be done with servers. These criteria would include measurable factors related to uptime, functionality, and performance to defined technical specifications.

The next thing that we can see in this section of the clause is that there is only a one year warranty, which in all likelihood is not nearly enough for this kind of purchase. There needs to be a warranty that at least covers three years for this kind of purchase. Ultimately, this particular issue is up to the discretion of the purchasing professional, but for something of this level of criticality, it is ideal to have a longer warranty period.

Let us now look at section (b) of this product warranty clause:

(b) Where during the Warranty Period the Goods or any part or unit thereof is found by the Buyer to be defective, the Seller shall at the written request of the Buyer, replace the same at the risk and expense (including transport costs and other incidental charges) of the Seller or if the Buyer agrees, make good or repair the same at the risk and expense (including transport costs and other incidental charges) of the Seller within 60 days from the date of the written demand from the Buyer to replace, make good or repair the same. The Goods or part or unit so replaced or repaired being then subject to the warranty for a further period of one (1) year from the date of receipt by the Buyer of the Goods or part of unit so replaced or repaired. If the Seller fails to make good or repair the Goods as stated herein, the Buyer reserves the right without prejudice to its other rights under the Contract or otherwise to buy such defective Goods from alternative sources or have the Goods repaired at alternative sources and all additional costs incurred thereby shall be recoverable from the Seller.

Once again, this is robust language for a general contract, and everything seems to read fine. However, think about what is being purchased here: servers for a financial services company. This section of the clause indicates that it will take as long as 60 days to remedy the problem. Can the financial services industry afford to have their client and corporate information housed inside a non-functional server for up to 60 days? Absolutely not! Further it does not specify calendar days or business days – the supplier may later argue that these were business days and not calendar days. In such case, the repair or replacement period would move from two months to three months! This would have to be modified to something much more aggressive – perhaps a 24 hour repair or replace set of terms, potentially along with guarantees about data backup and recovery.

The good news is that the Seller is agreeing to pay not only for the repair or replacement, but also for shipping. They are also allowing the Buyer to make the decision to repair or replace. The other issues raised above however make the clause completely unacceptable and in need of modification via amendment.

Let us now move onto the final section (c) of this product warranty clause:

(c) The Seller warrants that it will select and furnish personnel experienced and skilled in the type of work they are to perform under the Contract and that the Services to be performed under the Contract will be performed with due care and diligence and in a workmanlike manner within the turnaround time specified by the Buyer and in accordance with the Buyer's requirements. In the event the Services or part thereof do not conform to the requirements under the Contract, the Seller shall forthwith re-perform the Services. Until such time as the defective Services are re- performed to the satisfaction of the Buyer, the Buyer shall not be obliged to make payment therefore or, if payment has already been made, the Seller shall refund to the Buyer all sums paid.   Any additional or incidental costs related to the re-performance of the Services or part thereof shall be borne solely by the Seller.

What we can see here, among other things, is that the Seller provides assurances that experienced and skilled employees will work on remedying the defective product. Who however is determining if they are in fact experienced and skilled, and what is the definition of "experienced and skilled"? At a minimum, there needs to be language that says that the Buyer has the right to reject unskilled personnel and request replacement at the Supplier's expense. The term "workmanlike manner" is also undefined. By what criteria will the work be workmanlike? Normally, this will be called "*industry* workmanlike manner," which is meant to indicate that the work will at least be equivalent to industry standards, but the omission of the word "industry" makes things less clear in this case.

Additionally, we now have a conflict with a prior section of this clause. In section (b), there is a 60 day window to do the work, but in section (c), it now says the work will be done "within the turnaround time specified by the Buyer". It is unclear now which one of these time parameters will govern the agreement. Is it 60 days, or is it the Buyer defined turnaround time? Conflicting clauses invite debate, and for the purposes of contract breach, the supplier will surely argue that the 60 day period is the amount of time they should be held accountable to.

Finally, there is a provision whereby the supplier will re-perform services if there are still problems after their repair or replacement. This sounds good, except they do not specify what the time frame is for re-performing the work. Will it be done within the 60 day window? Does the clock start over? Is there no time frame at all when it comes to re-performing the warranty work? All of this is unclear and open to debate.

There are many other things that could be addressed in analyzing this clause (for instance, there is no talk of direct or consequential damages – what happens if there is a catastrophic data loss as a consequence of a product defect during the warranty period?), but we have covered the salient highlights. Keep in mind, it is very possible that this clause, in its original format and wording, would be perfectly acceptable to the legal department. Therefore, it should be abundantly clear that the legal department's approval does not mean that purchasing has a good business contract in their hands. As previously stated, it could still be a terrible contract for the business. Legal and purchasing are typically looking for different things (although everything that legal looks for has a direct correlation to TCO and purchasing professionals should pay close attention and exercise influence in this process), and these objectives should not be confused.

The key message from having done this exercise is this: standard contract clauses do not necessarily provide adequate protection, and approval from the legal department does not necessarily mean that this will be a good contract for the business. The other message of course is that failure to exercise proper diligence up front in such assessments will result in excessive time spent on the backend managing supplier excursions as a consequence. By that point, no actions purchasing can take will be preventative in nature. Every action taken will be reactive, by definition. It is our job to be proactive and not reactive in our professions.

Chapter IV: Analyzing Common Terms & Conditions

In this section, we will look at the most common clauses that
are addressed in long form contracts. What you need to do
right now, before reading any further, is to obtain a copy of
your company's long form goods and services contract
template. It is important to get a goods and services contract
template (and not a goods contract template or a services
contract template) because this combination template is likely
the most comprehensive standard contract template your
company has. As we go through each clause in this chapter, it
is imperative that you find the corresponding clause in your
corporate goods and services standard long form contract
template and analyze and internalize what the contents of this
chapter mean relative to what your firm's standard contract
language states. Doing so will greatly enable your progress,
results, and understanding as it pertains to contract terms
negotiations.

Now that you have a copy of your firm's long form goods and services standard contract template in hand, the methodology used to analyze these common contract clauses will be as follows: header, purpose of the clause, supplier's desired position, and your desired position.

The header is the name assigned to any particular clause in a contract. Different companies use different headers, but the most common headers will be used here. If a particular header does not look familiar, focus on the content of that clause as described in this book, and then associate this content back to the appropriate header and corresponding clause in your firm's long form contract template.

The analysis of the purpose of the clause will outline why this clause exists and what it is intended to accomplish. Finally, because many of the clauses have predictable reactions from suppliers, I am capturing the typical supplier desired position, as well as a recommended starting point for your desired position.

However, remember the disclaimer in the Preface of this book: this book is only a guide, and legal decisions should always be made after consulting with your internal management and legal department. The best decision for your firm and your circumstances may very well be different than what I am recommending, though I have tried to word the recommendations in such a way as to enable universal applicability.

The clauses that will be covered are as shown below:

A.   Term of agreement

B.   Definitions

C.   Warranty

D.   Packing and shipment

E.   Intellectual property

F.   Confidentiality

G.   Contract clause headers

H.   Compliance with laws/applicable law

I.   Damages

J.   Pricing

K.   Payment terms and invoicing

L.   Insurance

M.   Background check

N.   Limitation of liability

O.   Indemnification

P.   Force majeure/contingencies

Q.   Dispute resolution: arbitration, mediation, litigation

R.   Mergers/modifications/waivers

S.   Survival clauses

T.   Termination (cause, convenience)

U.   Contract components that aren't usually limited to one clause:

      a. Material and minor breach of contract

      b. Disclaimers

Now that the above list has been identified, we move onto review of each clause individually. As we go through these, you are encouraged to have a long form version of your firm's goods and services contract available for reference. This will reinforce the information conveyed and help make it immediately applicable in the context of your work environment.

A.   Term of agreement

Purpose of the clause: The term of agreement clause is meant to determine when the agreement starts and when it ends. The contract does not begin governance before this point, but it may end its governance after this point, at least for certain components. We will discuss this in the survival contract clause later. For now, we will go with the basic assumption that the contract governance period starts and ends with the dates noted on the agreement. It should be noted that a contract may be backdated and does not need to have a date associated with the exact date it was signed. Similarly, it may also be forward dated to a date in the future.

There is no right answer to how long a contract should be, as it depends entirely on the circumstances. The matrix below is intended to act as a guide in this decision making process.

Nature of Relationship with Supplier

	Non-Strategic	Strategic
Stable or decreasing	Shorter Agreement 1 – 3 years	Medium Agreement 3 +/- years
Volatile or Increasing	Medium Agreement 3 +/- years	Longer Agreement 3 – 5 years

Nature of Industry Price Climate

The basic message in the graphic above is that there are two primary drivers for longer term agreements: strategic relationships and an environment of volatile or increasing prices.

Strategic relationships encompass a myriad of circumstances. The relationship could be single or sole sourced, and critical from a supply line perspective. The relationship may be one in which there have been capital and/or human (time) investments made, and the switching costs of moving to another supplier are too high. The relationship may be one in which the items being purchased are of a strategic nature to the development or delivery of products for your firm. There may be intellectual property sharing arrangements that make the relationship strategic.

There are still many other reasons why this may be the case – the bottom line is that strategic relationships generally merit longer contracts, the reason being that the known time horizon for doing business with that supplier is longer.

The other category that merits longer term contracts is those deals that operate in an environment of volatile or increasing prices and there is desire in place to lock down pricing on a longer arrangement or to establish a supply pipeline that is solid at least several years into the future - in a market that likely has supply issues that are causing the price volatility.

The typical concerns with establishing longer term contracts are that a) it may put the purchasing professional in "supplier jail" for that length of time and/or b) the supplier will get content and lose their total cost edge. Neither one of these have to be true.

To address the first point, purchasing professionals should always have a termination for convenience clause (to be discussed later in this chapter) in their contracts, allowing them to exit "supplier jail" on demand. Secondly, having a contract for a stated period does not mean that the purchasing professional does not have the right to renegotiate pricing and hold regular supplier business reviews with scorecards in place that keep the supplier sharp and hungry. Finally, there is no rule that requires single sourcing arrangements, unless there is an exclusivity clause in the contract, which is definitely not standard in long form contract templates. More than one supplier can be qualified and utilized in most cases, providing both reduced supply line risk and ongoing price competitiveness. In the case of sole sourcing arrangements, the purchasing professional should consider development of a second source to reduce risk of supply interruptions and ensure ongoing TCO competitiveness.

In the end, the term of agreement is ultimately a business decision and may not completely follow the matrix above in all cases. It should be noted that in some cases, an evergreen term is agreed upon, whereby the contract never expires, unless a termination clause in the contract is exercised. This is usually reserved for such arrangements such as long term software agreements where most of the money was paid up front and long term maintenance support is required.

<u>Supplier's desired position</u>: in most cases, the supplier will want the longest term agreement possible. There is the very uncommon circumstance where industry demand for a supplier's product far exceeds supply, and therefore the supplier wants to opportunistically agree only to a shorter term agreement to not miss out on pricing opportunities in the market.

<u>Your desired position</u>: the *right* length of agreement, with the appropriate termination language in place (will be covered later in this agreement).

B.   Definitions

<u>Purpose of the clause</u>: the definitions clause is meant to provide very specific definitions to words or short phrases that are of significance in the contract that could otherwise be subject to varying interpretation. These words and short phrases are then defined in the definitions clause, and thereafter, the use of those words is always with a capitalized first letter, telling the

reader that this word is defined in the definitions clause of the contract.

A common example of this is the terms "buyer" and "seller". These are frequently defined as the actual firms that are doing the buying and selling respectively, as opposed to being defined as the actual individuals who are engaging in the corresponding contract activities. Any other term that may cause issues if interpreted in varying fashion should be predefined in the definitions clause. For instance, if 'product acceptance' is a critical part of the contract, it could be defined as "acceptance of the product as determined by written approval from an authorized Buyer representative." In defining it as such, it can simply be referred to as "Product Acceptance" elsewhere in the contract without having to explain in every instance, and also while still mitigating the risk that the supplier could find any other interpretation for the term product acceptance in the contract. This is one of those contract clauses where the purchasing professional and the seller generally have the same exact objectives: clarity of

contract terms. Rarely are the definitions negotiated in conflict

between the two parties.

Supplier's desired position: potentially ambiguous terms that

are of importance in the contract predefined to ensure a

common understanding.

Your desired position: potentially ambiguous terms that are of

importance in the contract predefined to ensure a common

understanding.

C.   Warranty

Purpose of the clause: the warranty clause is one of the most

misunderstood by purchasing professionals. There is the

common perception that a warranty is always a good thing, and

the only variable that matters is how long it is good for.

Nothing could be further from the truth. Purchasing

professionals must always remember, a warranty is only a

promise that something is true – this may or may not be

something that provides significant or sufficient protection for the purchasing professional; it all depends on the specific language used.

Remedy for breach of warranty becomes very important in this assessment process as well. Many consumers have bought products that failed under warranty, only to find that the remedy for breach of warranty is so arduous and costly (need to contact supplier and negotiate for a return materials authorization, special packaging and shipping requirements, along with requirement to pay for shipping and sometimes return shipping as well) that they just give up altogether.

The same is true for purchasing contract warranty language. Because the contract doesn't know what is being purchased, it will remain very generic on the language (recall the product warranty clause for servers that we previously reviewed). It may just state that the supplier warrants that the product will be free from defects for a period of three years (for instance), and that the supplier is responsible for any remedies required (repair and/or replacement). This leaves many questions unanswered still.

Let us take the example of a critical direct materials supplier for which the purchasing professional discovers that units received are found to be defective. Because the standard contract template doesn't know what you are buying, acquisition specific details regarding the remedy for breach of warranty may not be sufficient or sufficiently clear, beyond the fact that the part will be repaired or replaced if found defective during the warranty period.

Consider the following questions in this scenario above: Who will pay for the return of the defective parts? Who will pay for the shipment of the replacement parts? In what time frame will the parts be replaced? Even if defined, does this time frame (say, 36 hours) mean during business hours, business days, or calendar days? 36 hours could actually be five days if interrupted by one holiday and if interpreted as being measured during working hours only. If a supplier engineer needs to be sent out, in what time frame will this happen and who will pay for their travel costs? All of these sorts of questions need to be answered via an amendment to the standard warranty language in the contract. Since that same contract template could also be used to buy something entirely non-critical, such as office supplies, the default contract language does not get into this kind of detail above. It is the purchasing professional's responsibility to ensure that it does.

Purchasing professionals need to know that there are two types of warranty: express and implied. An express warranty is one that is expressly written as a part of the agreement between the parties. An implied warranty is one that is not written, but is implied based on reasonable expectations for a product. For instance, a normal car tire (i.e. one that is not bald or previously damaged) should not lacerate if it hits a small rock.

This level of protection need not be expressly written in the warranty, as it is implied under protections provided by the UCC. In fact, there are a series of UCC implied warranties, as noted below (suppliers may try to disclaim these – be on the lookout!):

- Warranty of Merchantability
- Warranty of Fitness for a Particular Purpose
- Warranty of Title
- Warranty of Non-Infringement

What this means is that the product being purchased must first be merchantable, meaning it is of average quality and multiple units compared to one another will be similar. Secondly, the product must be fit for a particular purpose, meaning that the supplier must state that the product is in fact usable and intended to be used for one or more particular purposes. Next, the supplier must warrant that they in fact have title to what is being sold. Finally, they must warrant non-infringement, meaning the product does not infringe on the intellectual property rights of any third parties.

While these UCC implied warranties provide some level of assurances, it is never desirable for a purchasing professional to rely on anything that is outside of the contract as a primary method of warranty coverage.

Supplier's desired position: Have a warranty that is limited by time, scope, expenditure coverage, and remedy options.

Your desired position: Have a custom warranty that spells out exactly what is provided, how this will be measured, who will pay, and how breach of warranty will be remedied, including supplier response time and total time frame to closure.

D.   Packing and shipment

Purpose of the clause: to clearly define how the goods will be transported, who bears the cost, who bears risk during transport, when title transfers, how the goods will be inspected, and how they will be accepted upon passing inspection. Among other things, this will necessitate the purchasing professional working with their own firm's logistics department and assess the total cost of owning the transportation of the products and having title transfer at the seller's dock vs having the supplier manage transport and have title transfer at the purchasing professional's dock. This involves assessing several primary factors: criticality of item being transported, complexity of shipment, lead time on item being purchased, type of transportation, cost of transportation, cost of insurance, and whether a delivery/delay incentive clause is needed in the contract if the supplier is to manage shipment to the customer's dock.

The criticality of the item being transported is important to assess because the purchasing professional must recognize the difference between an item being shipped that is in support of, say, office supplies vs an item being shipped that is necessary to manufacture and deliver product. If the total cost of customer managed shipment vs supplier managed shipment is about the same, it may make sense to take a supplier managed shipment approach, so that the supplier is entirely responsible for on time and undamaged shipment of the goods. Of course the purchasing professional will have already assessed the remedy for breach of on time delivery of undamaged working products, and will also have language in the contract added that provides appropriate remedies.

All risks associated with the shipping procedure are important to understand, because the item being shipped may have shipping requirements that impact TCO, such as requiring refrigeration, the possibility of damage if the item is tipped in any direction other than specified, and in the case of international deliveries, the requirement for the item to go through customs with complex paperwork and potential delays. In such cases, it may also make sense for the purchasing professional have the supplier manage transport, title, and risk of loss all the way to the customer dock.

The lead time for the item being purchasing is also important to understand, because if there is damage that takes place en route, the time to replacement needs to be comprehended by the purchasing professional. For very long lead time items, the purchasing professional once again may want to have the supplier own shipment, risk of loss, and title all the way to the customer dock, assuming the total cost is roughly the same when compared to having the purchasing professional manage shipping from the supplier's dock.

Once again, the remedy for breach of delivery dates (i.e. for delivery past the contractual due date or dates) needs to be written in a way to account for worst case scenarios – standard long form templates do not typically address this. If the item is are of high criticality or if the date of receipt is critical, there should be language included that indicates in what exact time frame and in what exact manner items that are damaged in shipment will be replaced by the supplier, possibly including reference to damages for late deliveries.

Such replacement deliveries can be at lead times that are much shorter than the normal schedule, necessitating that the supplier establish their own contingency plans to ready for such circumstances, which may mean that they need to have on-hand stock at all times in the event of such an emergency. This is important to assess because sometimes replacement with standard leadtimes or a simple return of money paid for these items is not sufficient to make the purchasing professional whole again, particularly if there are lost revenues or profits as a result of the delayed or damaged shipment.

The type of transportation proposed by both the supplier and the internal customer must be understood and dissected by the purchasing professional. If anything other than the lowest cost method of shipping is being used, then this is an immediate area that must be better understood, the reason being that more expensive shipping may be used by either the supplier and/or the internal customer to make up for lack of planning in the process. In such cases, all parties involved need to be challenged to understand why a particular product must be shipped overnight, by air instead of sea, or using a more expensive but faster route.

The purchasing professional must be persistent and cannot stop investigations by simply being told by either party of the criticality of the shipments being the motivating factor. Customers will often say "the money we save by getting this quicker is far more than the extra expense associated with expedited shipment". This answer at face value is not good enough justification, because it presumes that shipping is the only way to expedite the overall cycle time. The question must be asked "I need to understand what is preventing us from using a lower total cost method of shipment and placing the orders earlier, to ensure the same arrival date at our dock?

What can be done from an end to end business process perspective to cut the cycle time elsewhere instead of simply paying more for shipping?"

The purchasing professional must be relentless in understanding this business process angle, because in most but not all cases, the expedited shipment is to make up for a lack of planning somewhere in the supply chain, and expedited shipping is merely a symptom. The root cause needs to be understood and addressed wherever possible, ensuring no roadblocks to utilizing the lowest total cost methodology for shipment.

Assessing the cost of transportation is typically fairly simple, because the supplier should be required to outline this in their proposal, with the purchasing professional being sure that this is a total cost quotation with no hidden or extra costs involved. The purchasing professional can then go to the logistics department in their own firm and ask them two questions: 1)

How much would it cost us to manage freight, insurance, duty (if applicable), and any other costs exactly as noted on this supplier proposal for these items? 2) What is the lowest total cost method of shipping these items, independent of delivery timeframes?

The first question is asking what it would cost the purchasing professional's firm to do exactly what the supplier is proposing, and the second question is asking what the lowest total cost solution is for perhaps what *should be done*, assuming all supply chain planning issues are analyzed and addressed. From there, both total cost approaches can be compared with what the supplier is proposing and the purchasing professional can make a decision on how they wish to proceed, depending on the total cost opportunity at hand.

Cost of insurance is important for the purchasing professional to understand as well, as this may be a significant total cost component. The purchasing professional should ask their logistics department what the insurance cost would be on shipment if shipment was to be managed by the logistics department, using all the same parameters the supplier is recommending – unless there is reason to do otherwise.

A delivery/delay incentive is something that can be assessed and implemented by the purchasing professional to ensure on time and undamaged delivery of goods on or by a particular date. This will entail the predefinition of damages for late delivery or for delivery of damaged goods. This predefinition of damages is referred to as liquidated damages, because the damages are defined before the event itself takes place, if at all. The purchasing professional may for instance put language in the contract in the packing and shipment clause (vis a vis a contract amendment) that introduces a delivery/delay incentive, as shown in the example below:

"For every day that undamaged and working product is delivered after the Buyer defined delivery due date to

Customer dock on the Buyer's Purchase Order, Supplier shall provide Buyer with a price reduction of .5% on the products in question on said Purchase Order."

Note that this figure of .5% per day was not called a penalty, but rather a price reduction. This is a critically important point, because a penalty is a form of punitive damage, and only the courts can enforce punitive damages. Further, the courts will generally expect that if punitive damages are in fact introduced into contract language by the purchasing professional, there should also be equivalent incentive language in place as well.

In this case, that would mean providing a .5% price increase for every day in which the products are delivered early. This can amount to huge and unexpected "bonus" payments. The state of California discovered this they worked such a clause into a highway development contract in Sacramento, and got surprised when the supplier had their crews work around the clock to finish three months early, resulting in shocking and unexpected incentive payments in the millions to the contractor. From a TCO management perspective, it is better to avoid these situations entirely and focus on delivery/delay incentives that are price reduction focused only.

The following is a list of more commonly used contract freight terms that should be well understood by the purchasing professional (Source: Incoterms 2010, www.export.gov):

RULES FOR ANY MODE OF TRANSPORT:

ExWorks (EXW): the seller fulfills his obligations by having the goods available for the buyer to pick up at his premises or another named place (i.e. factory, warehouse, etc.). Buyer bears all risk and costs starting when he picks up the products at the seller's location until the products are delivered to his location. Seller has no obligation to load the goods or clear them for export.

Free Carrier (FCA): the seller delivers the goods export cleared to the carrier stipulated by the buyer or another party authorized to pick up goods at the seller's premises or another named place. Buyer assumes all risks and costs associated with delivery of goods to final destination including transportation after delivery to carrier and any customs fees to import the product into a foreign country.

Carriage Paid To (CPT): seller clears the goods for export and delivers them to the carrier or another person stipulated by the seller at a named place of shipment. Seller is responsible for the transportation costs associated with delivering goods to the named place of destination but is not responsible for procuring insurance.

Carriage and Insurance Paid To (CIP): seller clears the goods for export and delivers them to the carrier or another person stipulated by the seller at a named place of shipment. Seller is responsible for the transportation costs associated with delivering goods and procuring minimum insurance coverage to the named place of destination.

Delivered at Terminal (DAT): seller clears the goods for export and bears all risks and costs associated with delivering the goods and unloading them at the terminal at the named port or place of destination. Buyer is responsible for all costs and risks from this point forward including clearing the goods for import at the named country of destination.

Delivered at Place (DAP): seller clears the goods for export and bears all risks and costs associated with delivering the goods to the named place of destination not unloaded. Buyer is responsible for all costs and risks associated with unloading the goods and clearing customs to import the goods into the named country of destination.

Delivered Duty Paid (DDP): seller bears all risks and costs associated with delivering the goods to the named place of destination ready for unloading and cleared for import.

RULES FOR SEA AND INLAND WATERWAY TRANSPORT:

Free Alongside Ship (FAS): seller clears the goods for export and delivers them when they are placed alongside the vessel at the named port of shipment. Buyer assumes all risks/costs for goods from this point forward.

Free on Board (FOB): seller clears the goods for export and delivers them when they are onboard the vessel at the named port of shipment. Buyer assumes all risks/cost for goods from this moment forward.

Cost and Freight (CFR): seller clears the goods for export and delivers them when they are onboard the vessel at the port of shipment. Seller bears the cost of freight to the named port of destination. Buyer assumes all risks for goods from the time goods have been delivered on board the vessel at the port of shipment.

Cost, Insurance, and Freight (CIF): seller clears the goods for export and delivers them when they are onboard the vessel at the port of shipment. Seller bears the cost of freight and insurance to the named port of destination. Seller's insurance requirement is only for minimum cover. Buyer is responsible for all costs associated with unloading the goods at the named port of destination and clearing goods for import. Risk passes from seller to buyer once the goods are onboard the vessel at the port of shipment.

Supplier's desired position: generally speaking, to have an arrangement that maximizes profit while also shifting as much risk to the purchasing professional as possible. This may involve having ownership for the shipping process as a core profit strategy, while having limited liability for late or damaged delivery of goods.

Your desired position: to have an arrangement that is the lowest TCO for your firm, while ensuring the risk is borne by the right parties for any issues that occur before, during, and after title transfer. This also includes ensuring contract language that requires the supplier prepare and pack items for shipment in a manner that follows good commercial practice, is acceptable to common carriers for shipment at the lowest rate, and is adequate to ensure safe arrival. As aforementioned, this also involves ensuring that expedited and more costly shipping methods are not being used to compensate for lack of planning somewhere in the supply chain.

E.   Intellectual property (IP)/new developments

Purpose of the clause: to ensure that all previously developed IP is owned by the supplier with no third party interests that may present conflict and to ensure any new IP developed in the course of the agreement has a clear and rightful owner, usually the purchasing professional's firm, unless there are compelling reasons for arrangements otherwise.

The topic of IP is so complex and so critical and so situation specific that it cannot be adequately addressed in a simple section of this book. Legal department involvement is always advised when this topic is being discussed or negotiated with suppliers. The following table will help identify the various types of IP:

	Copyright	Patent	Trademark	Trade Secret	Other
What is protected	"original works of authorship"	products, processes	business identities	business secrets	design patents, chip masks, databases
Symbols	©	Patented...	™, SM, ®		(m)
Registration	Library of Congress	Patent Office	Patent Office		
Tests	originality (implicit)	unique, novel, non-obvious	does not duplicate existing mark		
How obtained	Publication (registration)	Examination by PTO	Registration with PTO, common law	Create secret	
Duration	Most cases: Life of author + 70 yrs	The longer of 20 years from filing or 17 years from issuance	while in use	while secret	

One of the things that the purchasing professional needs to watch for is internal customer behavior as it relates to IP. Internal customers must be educated on what IP is, how it can arise, why it is valuable, and how to protect it. There also may need to be decisions about who will own any such IP – although the default should always be that the purchasing entity should own any IP that arises during the course of the agreement.

To reference a real case, there was a motherboard manufacturing company that had an engineer who worked with a supplier of manufacturing floor thermal ovens and gave them the idea to have a different type of gas go into the thermal chamber to improve attach rate and yields for the motherboards. It was such a good idea that not only did the supplier do this for that engineer's manufacturing lines, but also for all their other customers. The engineer did not realize that he had created intellectual property with this idea and that he allowed the supplier to benefit from it. This is not just of financial consequence, but there is also the issue that the competition of this company would also benefit from this innovation. Now there was a problem.

Once purchasing found out about these activities, action needed to be taken. Everything above was verified, and then the customer was informed of how IP can arise and how it should not be freely communicated or given away without internal due diligence first. As it turns out, this company did not want to be in the motherboard business. They had many other product lines, and they made almost no money on motherboards. They were only in this business by necessity, to ensure their microprocessors had a platform to land on when they entered the marketplace. Therefore, it was one of those rare circumstances where if the competition (other motherboard manufacturers) benefitted from this IP, so did this company, because it would help them get out of the business, or at least keep them from having to grow it.

The next step was to decide how to establish IP ownership and also to ensure there was a beneficial financial arrangement put in place in return for this IP innovation. The legal team was involved and the supplier was given IP rights to the thermal oven innovation. Purchasing was involved as well and negotiated a steep discount on all future oven purchases in return. It was a win/win all the way around – the supplier got to benefit from the IP, the industry marketplace of motherboard manufacturers was enabled, and the customer group was able to purchase future product at a steep discount in return. The key to all of this, however, was the recognition of IP development and action taken to ensure ownership and any resultant benefits were clearly established.

The purchasing professional needs to understand that either party can come into a contract owning IP that will be used, or they can jointly develop IP during the course of the agreement, or they can independently create IP during the course of the agreement. It is also important to note that the creation of IP can be incidental or even accidental. In the cases where either party comes into a contract with existing ownership of IP, they should continue to own that IP. Should IP be developed over the course of the contract term, there needs to be up front agreement over who will own that IP. Just paying for it does not guarantee ownership. Neither does being the designer of that IP. The most important determinant is how the contract itself is written from an IP perspective.

Supplier's desired position: exclusive rights and ownership of all IP developed under the course of the agreement, in addition to ownership of all previous technologies for which the supplier already owned the IP or is in the process of establishing ownership of such (e.g., patent pending).

Your desired position: supplier owns all previously developed technologies, no third party IP infringements, purchasing professional firm has exclusive rights and ownership of all IP developed under the course of this agreement in any capacity, supplier will aid purchasing professional's firm in formally establishing this IP ownership.

F.   Confidentiality/publicity

Purpose of the clause: Major firms spend millions, and in some cases billions, to carefully craft and develop their corporate image, reputation, and goodwill in industry and the community. It is a critical part of their marketing and legal strategies as a company. The ways in which the company's name, trademarks, and brands are used in the public realm – in any capacity – are carefully managed as a part of this process.

Suppliers often if not always want to use a customer's name (the name of the company for which the purchasing professional works) in advertising, brochures, verbal presentations, presentation documents, corporate proxy documents, etc. The message is "look at who chose to work with us." Several potential problems can arise as a result of this kind of supplier action.

The first problem is that there can be the perception that the customer firm is *endorsing* the supplier's firm. Endorsements are very carefully crafted arrangements, performed under very specific and well defined circumstances. They generally must go through numerous approval bodies on both sides (customer and supplier), before the exact nature of the endorsement is exactly understood, agreed to, and monitored. Having the supplier unilaterally use the customer's name in such a capacity without going through this process can be highly problematic. It is in fact very possible that the customer does not want to endorse the supplier's product or service, for reasons of policy or for reasons related to their actual satisfaction levels with these goods or services.

The second problem is that the customer's company may not want the very existence of the agreement between the two companies to be made public in any capacity. This can be considered company confidential information that gives the customer's company a competitive edge in some capacity. It may also leak information to the competition regarding what suppliers are used and in what capacity.

The third problem is that the use of the customer's trademark and brand information and intellectual property may result in incorrect or unapproved display models. Most large companies have a branch of their legal department that exclusively exists to ensure the proper and exact correct utilization of the company's trademark and brands, both internally and externally. The trademarks and brands must be displayed correctly, with the correct size, color, placement, and because most firms have many trademarks and brands, the correct versions must be used for each instance.

If a supplier unilaterally decides to put this information into any sort of documentation, then this customer trademarks and brands control process is bypassed completely, and the probability for error is high. Even if everything is done correctly, there is still the probability that what is correct today is not correct sometime in the future, because of the evolving nature of a company's trademarks and brands, which can change over time.

The fourth problem is that there may be the appearance that the customer's firm is in a joint advertising agreement with the supplier, if in fact that is how the customer's name is used. This has obvious implications, and the customer group's marketing department may take exception to this.

One other thing this clause is meant to accomplish is to outline exactly how confidential information is transmitted during the course of the agreement. For instance, the customer's firm may need to communicate future product information to a supplier. This is very confidential information, because it may not be public yet. This contract clause typically calls for a specific legal process to be followed in which the specific information conveyed is either captured under the umbrella of an NDA (Non-Disclosure Agreement) or both captured by NDA and then in addition is expressly articulated in a legal confidential information transmittal form and signed by authorized representatives of both parties before the information is released. These forms will then contractually prevent the parties from disclosing this to any other third party without written approval from an authorized representative of the firm that originally disclosed this information. This clause will often and usually does survive the length of the actual agreement. This will be addressed when we get to the clause that is entitled "survivals."

<u>Supplier's desired position</u>: The supplier's desired position will almost always be to freely use the customer's name in any and all kind of communications, especially those that are external to their firm, in an effort to demonstrate the legion of customers that have bought from them.   However, the supplier will typically be in agreement with the NDA process for communicating confidential information.

<u>Your desired position</u>: Control exactly how your firm's name is used in all capacities by the supplier and ensure confidential information is transmitted via your firm's corporate confidential information transmittal legal process.

It is important to remember that in some cases, authorized representatives from your company may actually find it acceptable for the supplier to use your company's name in advertising or in other capacities. If this is worth something to the supplier, and may help them somehow improve their business model in some value added capacity, it is entirely

within your right to include this in the negotiation process and

only grant this right in return for a commensurate discount in

price or reduction in total cost (increased warranty, improved

customer support model, etc).

G.   Contract clause headers

Purpose of the clause: This contract clause is usually entitled

something like "headers" or "headings" or "subject headers" or

the like. Every clause or series of clauses in a contract falls

under a header that is nothing more than a categorical

description for what type of information is contained in the

clauses that follow. This clause merely indicates that the

subject headers for the various contract clauses do not have any

inherent legal meaning or implication in and of themselves and

that only the words in the actual clauses themselves (and not in

their subject headers) have legal significance.

<u>Supplier's desired position</u>: Typically, on this topic, suppliers will want the same contract language as is contained in your standard purchasing contract. On very rare occasion, a supplier may want to use this clause to their advantage by having pleasant or misleading contract clause headers. For instance, to cite a real example where a supplier had nefarious intent, there was a supplier contract with a contract clause entitled "indemnification by seller," however, the actual contract clause contained verbiage that indicated *indemnification by the buyer*, not the seller. This was technically allowed, since the contract contained the aforementioned headers contract clause.

Purchasing professionals should always be on alert, ensuring that they are focusing on the language in the clauses and not the language in the headers.

<u>Your desired position</u>: Have headings that accurately describe the clause contents, as they should already be presented in your existing standard contract templates.

H.   Compliance with laws

<u>Purpose of the clause</u>: To ensure that two primary things are clear: that the laws of the state in which the contract in question shall be governed, as well as the requirement for the supplier to act in accordance with all applicable laws for the jurisdictions in which they support in fulfilling their contractual obligations for the customer.

The purchasing professional in the United States may have a contract governed by the laws of any state which their legal department specifies. Normally, the most desirable states to have a contract governed in are New York, California, and Delaware. The reason for this is that the courts in these states are the ones that are most likely to use the "four corners rule," whereby the contract itself is used as the greatest factor in determining interpretation and enforcement in a court of law, as opposed to researching and relying up on course of past conduct by either or both parties, or referencing industry standard practices in either the buyer or the seller's industry.

Having the laws governed under the laws of one of these states then places the actual contract language in a stronger position if disagreements or conflicts are ever taken to court. This of course can be a liability if the contract was poorly written, incomplete, or not reflective of actual business practice between the parties – which is why the focus in this book is one writing contracts correctly, the first time.

Supplier's desired position: Generally speaking, the supplier will want the contract to be governed under the laws of the state in which they are headquartered or operate their sales office out of. Most suppliers do not have issue agreeing to the laws of New York, Delaware, or California however.

<u>Your desired position</u>: New York, Delaware, and California remain my most preferred options for reasons stated above, but you should absolutely check with your legal department to ascertain their preferences. When choosing the governing law/jurisdiction for your contract, your legal counsel will consider the following factors: Backlog of trial docket, rules of evidence in a given jurisdiction, and relative sophistication of judge and jury selection process. Every state has acceptable laws and practices, with the exception of Louisiana, which still has not adopted UCC fully the way the other states have, and they still have French code influence in their laws. Both of these reasons make it a good idea to have your contracts governed by any state other than Louisiana, unless your legal department cautions or directs you otherwise, in which case you should follow their direction exclusively.

I.   Material and minor breach of contract

<u>Purpose of the clause</u>: In actuality, this is not usually a clause in the contract, but it should be something that inserted in the right areas, and should be recognized when inserted by the supplier as proposed language.

A minor breach of contract is one in which there is a partial or immaterial breach where there *has been* substantial performance against the outlined contract requirements for consideration. A material breach of contract therefore is a failure to perform by one party in which substantial performance against the outlined contract requirements for consideration are not made, in such a fashion that the matter is actionable (i.e. can be taken to court).

An example of material vs. minor breach is as follows. Assume a very large billboard is ordered with very specific verbiage and graphics. It arrives exactly as designed, except the border of the billboard graphic is a slightly lighter color blue than what was requested – almost unnoticeably different, yet still slightly off. The color blue in this case was an arbitrary color and not a company color that has any level of marketing or legal significance. It can be said then that this may in fact be a minor breach of contract, because consideration was fulfilled in a substantial manner.

Now if the company logo was painted in the wrong color blue, this would clearly be a material breach of contract. To eliminate all doubt, the purchasing professional could add language in the contract that states something along the lines of "failure to provide an exact depiction on the billboards of graphics provided by Buyer shall result in a material breach of contract. Buyer shall have exclusive authority to determine the extent to which this was accomplished successfully. Should Buyer notify Supplier of any material breach of contract in this regard, Supplier shall provide a replacement billboard to Buyer's exact specifications with 48 hours of notification, at Supplier's expense."

Note once again that the standard contract template does not call out breach of any clause a material or minor breach, because the template doesn't know what is being purchased. It is the job of the purchasing professional to call out material and minor breaches in the contract. In reality, all that needs to be called out are those areas that are material breaches. This will capture the supplier's attention and the attention of their legal team.

For instance, take the example of a construction contract whereby a concrete supplier is to pour concrete foundation on a particular day. If they come one day late, they may argue that this is only a minor breach of contract while the purchasing professional may view this as a material breach of contract because the construction schedule has now slipped by one day, resulting in a domino type effect to the whole schedule. What leverage does the purchasing professional have after the fact to try and prove that a breach is in fact a material breach instead of a minor breach of contract?

The problem of course is that designation of a contract breach as material means nothing if there is not an outlined definition for what the remedy for breach of contract is. This can be addressed either with language that implies the level of contract breach or language that expressly states it, along with language that specifies the remedy for breach of contract. For instance, when a contract says "time is of the essence for all product deliveries," the contract is making the implication that late deliveries shall constitute a material breach of contract. It is better, however, to expressly state (in this example) "failure to deliver products on time shall be constitute a material breach of contract."

However, simply stating that failure to perform to a particular contract clause criteria is a material breach of contract is insufficient. The goal is to not only identify areas of required performance and compliance, but to also specify the remedy if there is failure to do so. Therefore, it is ideal to have a remedy indicated as well. Failure to include a remedy for a material breach of any clause means that the purchasing professional must still reactively respond to every such breach and negotiate a resolution – at the worst possible time – after the supplier already has the business in hand and after the excursion has already taken place. The best time to negotiate this is when the supplier is trying to get the business, and before any excursions ever take place.

As an example of the above, the product delivery clause above can be modified to read) "failure to deliver products on time shall be constitute a material breach of contract. For every calendar day in which products are delivered past Buyer communicated due date shall result in a .5% discount given by Supplier to Buyer." Now the purchasing professional only needs to ensure the supplier does what they are supposed to, which is to give an additional discount, when products are delivered late. Note that this remedy can be anything it takes to make the purchasing professional whole again. The focus should not be on profiteering, but rather, just being made whole again. If there is cost of cover incurred due to late deliveries, the supplier can be made responsible for this. If there are other damages incurred, the supplier can be made contractually liable for these as well (so long as they agree).

The ultimate goal in all of this, however, is to ensure supplier performance to contract – not to try and benefit from supplier failure to do so. In such cases where the supplier does not perform, the resolution should ideally already be spelled out in the contract, thus saving much time and heartache.

Supplier's desired position: The supplier will want nothing to be defined as material or minor breach in the contract, but will welcome or may try to insert language that states "time is of the essence in making payments." This is a very subtle mechanism to convey that not paying them on time equates to a material breach of contract. As remedy for breach of contract, they will often times also provide stipulations for penalties for paying late. Purchasing professionals are highly encouraged to never sign a contract that has penalties associated with late payment. The response I have found most powerful is to simply state that your A/P (Accounts Payable) department will not pay late payment penalties, or that your company has a corporate policy against them and does not deviate from this position.

Your desired position: To put "teeth" in every important clause in the contract against which you need to see substantial performance by defining those areas as being a material breach of contract if not performed to in full against your documented expectations. Remedy for breach of contract should also be defined in such cases. Minor breach of contract need not be defined, as everything else that is a component of consideration that is not labeled as a material breach of contract will normally get interpreted as therefore being a minor breach of contract.

The amount of time you will save by pre-setting expectations in this manner (avoiding issues by stating clear expectations and also consequences for not meeting these expectations) and also by having the remedy for excursions pre-defined is immeasurable. In the vast majority of cases, purchasing professionals don't take this simple insurance measure, and as a consequence, often find themselves mired in managing supplier performance excursions that were either avoidable or easily remedied with little involvement on their part. This point cannot be emphasized enough.

J.   Damages

Purpose of the clause: This is another clause that is rarely a clause in and of itself. Damages are usually defined in the individual clauses in which damages are specified. There are several common types of legal damages that purchasing professionals need to know about. These are direct, consequential, and liquidated damages. There are other types of damages (indirect, incidental), but because those are less often seen in contracts, the focus will remain on the three damage types outlined above.

For all definitions below, we will assume a piece of capital equipment purchased for use in a manufacturing line that produces finished goods for sale to retailers and consumers. Note that the repeated use of this example is intentional, because of the criticality that such procurement brings about – non-functional equipment means the company cannot produce product, which is about the worst possible scenario for most any manufacturing company. The reader can and should take the knowledge from this and other such examples and apply it to their specific areas of purchase.

Let's assume that this piece of equipment malfunctions while under warranty, causing the manufacturing line it is in to be down for a period of two weeks – the period of time the supplier takes to remedy the issue.   We will then break down how the different types of damages covered will apply in this scenario.

Direct damages are those that take place in similar time and location to the incident. In this particular case, the direct damages are to the piece of equipment and to any product that were in it at the moment in which it malfunctioned. If the damage was electrical and it extended to other electrical items to which it was connected at that same moment, then this would also be considered a direct damage. Similarly, any damage caused to property and plant as an immediate result of this malfunction would be considered a direct damage.

In certain instances, a low expenditure supplier can have liability for a huge amount of direct damages. Though unrepresentative, take the example of the 1986 Space Shuttle Challenger explosion that was due to faulty o-rings (actually, it was due to poor testing procedures for o-rings, but let us assume for this example that the actual o-rings were defective). Chances are that these o-rings cost very little, when compared to the cost of that entire space shuttle (not to mention that seven crew members lost their life as a result). Direct damages would likely exceed one billion dollars – something that would put all but the largest suppliers on earth out of business completely. It is no surprise that suppliers are worried about potential damages that may arise during the course of a contract.

A consequential damage would be damages that do not take place in a similar time and place to the original incident, but take place as a direct result (as a consequence) of the incident. An example of this would be the fact that there would be two

139

weeks of lost profits associated with having manufacturing downtime while the capital equipment was awaiting repair or replacement by the supplier. Other consequential damages may include necessary follow up actions that were required to take place as a consequence of the malfunction, for instance bringing in additional crew or paying overtime to manage the handling of work in process units and resultant communications to customers whose orders will be late. Consequential damages can put suppliers out of business, in large part because that is where lost profits can be assessed, and lost profits in some businesses can add up to millions of dollars in a very short period of time.

Liquidated damages are those damage types that are monetarily predefined in the contract. An example of this is a delivery/delay incentive, which was previously covered in this book as well. A delivery/delay incentive may provide for an incentive (e.g., bonus payment) for early delivery of a good or service, as well as a disincentive (e.g., price reduction) for late delivery of the same good or service. This pre-definition of the price reduction for every day the good or service is delivered late is in fact a form of liquidated damage, because the damage is defined before the breach ever takes place – if in fact it ever takes place at all. Just having that language there will help prevent such occurrences, because the supplier knows full well what the consequence will be in the event of such an excursion.

As previously mentioned in this book, liquidated monetary damages should always be stated as a "price reduction" as opposed to a "penalty" in the contract; the reason being that punitive damages are the jurisdiction of the court and not the purchasing professional, and the court may only find such clauses enforceable if there is a corresponding incentive payment made available for performance that also exceeds stated contract expectations (such as delivering a product or service early). It is better to avoid all of this by not using the word "penalty" in any capacity when defining liquid damages.

<u>Supplier's desired position</u>: The supplier will want to introduce a clause in the contract entitled "Limitation of liability." This clause will then seek to put caps (limits) on the amount of liability that your firm can pursue and the supplier can be held liable for. Most typically, they will want to limit direct damages to the value of the contract and disclaim consequential damages altogether. Liquidated damages will often go completely unaddressed by the supplier (unless they have issue with liquidated damages proposed by the purchasing professional), with the exception of the supplier wanting to include language that enforces penalties for late payment, which we covered previously.

<u>Your desired position</u>: This is a unique contract clause that is virtually unlike all others, because the purchasing professional in this case should remain silent on the issue of direct damages, consequential damages, and limitation of liability. Liquidated damages of course by definition are not something the

142

purchasing professional can stay silent on, as conspicuous definition and documentation of liquidated damages is a firm requirement.

The reason which the purchasing professional should stay silent on the topics of direct damages, consequential damages, and limitation of liability is that this means by default that all damage types apply and there are no limits to what level of damages can be pursued, so long as the focus is on making the purchasing professionals' firm whole again. Anything beyond that is again in the realm of punitive damages, which the courts enforce in order to both punish and make an example of the offending party. This is the court's jurisdiction and should not be attempted to be covered when developing a contract.

If the purchasing professional is faced with the situation whereby the supplier wants to cap direct and/or consequential damages, the first thing that has to happen is that a risk assessment needs to be done. The purchasing professional needs to understand a worst case scenario of what can go wrong with the purchase transaction, and what the implications may be from a damages perspective. Then the purchasing professional needs to determine the expected benefit of proceeding with this supplier. In some cases, such as with a critical sole source supplier, there may be no choice but to proceed with a limitation of liability. In most cases though, the purchasing professional should be able to investigate viable alternatives to determine the business need to proceed with a limitation of liability with the supplier in question.

Ultimately, the purchasing professional's job in this case is not to make the decision, but to gather the necessary information and options to support decision making. Typically, a representative from the legal department and a very senior manager in the customer chain must buy off on any limitations of liability. The senior manager in the customer's department must have budgetary or corporate authority that is equivalent to the potential loss due to a limitation of liability clause, and the reason is that their division is likely the one that will pay for any such expenses, based on the risk they chose to undertake to support their business unit objectives. The legal department must typically also approve, as this is clearly a legal matter as well. The legal department may also include the risk management department in doing their analysis and assessment.

In most cases, where a limitation of liability is approved by both legal and the customer chain, it is expressed in terms of either a fixed figure or the value of the contract or in multitudes of the value of the contract. There are many possible outcomes. Direct damages could be unlimited (no limitation of liability) but consequential damages can be disclaimed altogether. Or both could be limited to the value of the contract in aggregate, or each could be individually limited to the value of the contract, or each to twice or three times the value of the contract, etc. The only limit to how limitation of liability can be structured is the author's creativity. Needless

to say, the less financially restrictive the limitation of liability

language is, the better for the purchasing professional.

K.   Pricing

<u>Purpose of the clause</u>: This clause is intended to identify where

in the contract pricing related terms are contained (with

expectation for compliance), to clarify any tax related

provisions where applicable, and to establish an MFC (Most

Favored Customer) provision – though actual terminology to

describe this concept varies from contract to contract.

Pricing related terms are often not actually in this pricing

contract clause, if for no other reason that the amount of

pricing related terms can and usually is voluminous. This

information is generally contained in an addendum to the

contract, and it may simply be a supplier's accepted pricing

quotation. Actual prices can be referenced or a discount

schedule can be referenced. There may also be a provision for no increases to list price during the course of the contract (which would increase prices paid if working off of a discount schedule). Having this information in an addendum instead of in the pricing clause itself also makes it easier to make pricing schedule amendments to the contract at a future date.

Some contracts contain tax related provisions in this pricing section as well. Typically, tax language in this clause may cover a number of topics. These often include the following types of stipulations:

- Pricing schedule not including taxes: The amounts to be paid by Buyer to Seller do not include any taxes.

- Seller is responsible for their own taxes: Buyer is not liable for any taxes that Seller is legally obligated to pay, including, but not limited to net income or gross receipts taxes, franchise taxes, and property taxes.

- Buyer will pay taxes due by law: Buyer will pay Seller any sales, use or value added taxes it owes due to this Agreement and which the law requires Seller to collect from Buyer.

- Buyer tax exemptions and tax indemnification: If Buyer provides Seller a valid exemption certificate, Seller will not collect the taxes covered by such certificate. Seller will indemnify and hold Buyer harmless from any claims, costs (including reasonable attorneys' fees) and liabilities that relate to Seller's taxes.

- Buyer tax withholdings: If the law requires Buyer to withhold taxes from payments to Seller, Buyer may withhold those taxes and pay them to the appropriate taxing authority. Buyer will deliver to Seller an official receipt for such taxes. Buyer will use reasonable efforts to minimize any taxes withheld to the extent allowed by law.

The MFC clause (which may be called "Competitive Pricing" or be given some other header in the pricing section of the contract) is intended to ensure that the pricing given by the supplier to the purchasing professional is either the best pricing given to any customer irrespective of volume or consistent with the best pricing given to any customer for "like volumes".

There is a dramatic difference between these two MFC clause variations. In the first one ("irrespective of volume"), this means that the supplier must offer their very best pricing, ostensibly reserved for only their biggest customers, even if only a few units are being purchased by the purchasing professional. In the second variant ("like volumes"), the supplier must at least match the best pricing being given to other customers who are buying similar quantities.

Supplier's desired position: The supplier will generally only want the pricing schedule to be accurate and clear and will also agree to the taxation language above, as it is industry standard and only clarifies and documents what should already be understood. The supplier will unequivocally want the MFC clause to be for like volumes and not independent of volume, with the exception being where the purchasing professional's anticipated volume will make them one of the supplier's largest customers.

Your desired position: The purchasing professional should strive for the same price and tax objectives as the supplier: clear pricing models, tax accountability with the right parties, and minimization of taxes while being fully compliant with all laws and regulations. The purchasing professional should, after consulting with internal counsel, strive to achieve MFC pricing independent of volume. It is important to be internally aligned with legal on this first because a very small number of companies have self imposed concerns about MFC with independent volumes, for fear of potential perceptions of antitrust. The author is not aware of any salient case law that supports this concern. The back fall position should then be MFC for like volumes.

It should be noted however that any MFC clause, regardless of variant, must have audit rights for the purchasing professional in order to be effective. Typically, this would be written such that the purchasing professional has the right to use a third party professional auditor to audit the supplier's compliance to the MFC, at the purchasing professional's expense. However, an additional stipulation is included that, should there be any findings, the supplier is then responsible not only for repayment of all MFC compliance gaps identified, but also for any and all costs associated with the audit itself. As for notification of impending audit, the desired language is typically such that purchasing may initiate such an audit with "reasonable notice," which allows for urgency of audit where circumstances may merit.

L.   Payment terms and invoicing

<u>Purpose of the clause</u>: The intention with this clause is to clarify the specific requirements and processes for how payment and invoicing will take place between the parties, as well as any associated early payment discount schedule that may be available. This clause will specify invoicing methods and requirements, length of time allotted for payment, how this length of time will be measured, payment methods, and a provision that payment does not constitute acceptance.

This clause will typically outline the content requirements for the supplier's invoice as well as where and how it should be sent (where in the case of a physical hard copy invoice and how in the case of an electronically transmitted invoice). It will also outline payment timelines and any early payment discounts. This is typically noted as with the following example: 2/10 Net 45, which means that if the supplier is paid within ten (10) days, the purchasing professional may take a two (2) percent discount, or in the alternative, and at the purchasing professional's sole discretion, the full amount may be paid in 45 days.

This period of time after which payment is made must also be clarified, in terms of when the "clock" starts and when it stops. In most cases, it is defined as starting when the purchasing professional's company (more specifically, the accounts payable department) receives an acceptable invoice that complies with all contract defined criteria, and it is defined as ending when payment transmission is made. If this whole process is done via mail, then a 45 day payment term could in fact become +/- 55 days, once postal time frames are accounted for. Similarly, if the invoice is not accepted for some reason, or if the supplier sends it to the wrong department (usually this means to the internal customer or to the purchasing professional) instead of to the accounts payable department, this will add to the time lag, because the accounts payable department must receive an acceptable invoice in order for the payment clock to start.

There is also typically a provision that indicates that payment does not constitute acceptance. This allows the purchasing professional to retain rights to identify and pursue resolution for product or service issues that are identified post-payment.

Supplier's desired position: The supplier in most cases will be in agreement with all provisions in this clause with the exception of two areas: One is they would prefer the clock to start upon sending of the invoice (not the receipt of an acceptable invoice) and for the clock to end upon receipt of payment (not the transmission of payment). Neither of these will be an issue however if the process is performed electronically. The second concern is the actual payment terms. They would prefer to receive their money as soon as possible, with little or no discounts offered for early payment.

For instance, an ideal for most suppliers would be 1/10 Net 30. Of course they would prefer payment upon receipt, but this is just not industry standard practice except in the most rare of exceptions.

Your desired position: The purchasing professional should aspire to negotiate the best payment terms possible and to not deviate from how accounts payables defines when the contract starts and stops – this should not be negotiable. The industry standard for payment terms has been increasing. Whereas 20 years ago 1/10 Net 30 or 2/10 Net 30 was the norm, now 1/10 Net 60 or 2/10 Net 60 is the norm. This is in large part due to the fact that most all invoicing and payment transmissions are done electronically, and so the payment window has been increased to keep the total payment cycle about the same for the purchasing professional's accounts payable department.

The purchasing professional should be familiar with what their company's weighted average cost of capital (WACC) is. The finance department should have this information. This is, in a nutshell, what the company earns on their money in the bank and in other liquid investments. If for instance the WACC for a given company is 6% annually, then this amounts to .5% per month. This means that any discounts given for early payment must exceed .5% per month to be worthy of consideration – anything less is a loss to the company.

To take a specific example, let us say that a supplier offers a 1/10 Net 40 payment term model. The purchasing professional could obtain a 1% discount by paying 30 days early. Since 1% extra cash in the bank exceeds the .5% WACC opportunity loss above, it would make financial sense to take the early payment discount, and in fact the saved .5% (1% discount minus .5% WACC opportunity loss for that same period) could be claimed as savings. It is worthy of mention however that many and perhaps most purchasing professionals would claim the entire 1% discount as their savings, although the true savings to the company is the residual .5% noted above in this scenario.

M.   Insurance

Purpose of the clause: The reason for this clause is to specify insurance types and insurance levels required by the purchasing professional's firm for the supplier in question. These factors (insurance type and amount of coverage needed) are entirely specific to the company, the industry, the supplier, whether or not services will be performed, whether or not hazardous or potentially hazardous work will be involved, whether or not work will be done on-site at the purchasing professional's facility, and any other perceived risk factors for that purchase scenario. The types of insurance that are more commonly seen are as follows (Source: Reuters, 2013):

Commercial general liability insurance - A standard insurance policy issued to business organizations to protect them against liability claims for bodily injury and property damage arising out of premises, operations, products, and completed operations.

Professional liability insurance pays for losses resulting from injuries to third parties when a professional's conduct falls below the profession's standard of care. For example, if a doctor makes a mistake that other doctors of his specialty would not have made, his patient might sue him. A malpractice policy will pay his defense costs and any judgment or settlement. Malpractice insurance is available for doctors, dentists, accountants, real estate agents, architects, and other professionals.

Commercial Automobile Insurance cover the cars, vans, trucks and trailers used in the supplier's business. The coverage will reimburse the supplier if their vehicles are damaged or stolen or if the driver injures a person or property.

Workers' compensation insurance covers a supplier for on-the-job injuries by their employees. Businesses with employees are required by various state laws to carry some type of workers' compensation insurance. In most cases, workers' compensation laws prohibit the employee from bringing a negligence lawsuit against an employer for work-related injuries.

The clause typically also requires that certificates of insurance are provided to the purchasing professional and that the purchasing professional's company is included on the certificate as an additional insured. Having an additional insured endorsement makes the purchasing professional's company an actual "insured" under the vendor's policy. This provides for full rights to coverage for losses arising out of the goods or services that the supplier provides, necessitates that the insurer must notify the purchasing professional of any material changes to, or cancellation of, the policy, and if an injured party makes a claim against the purchasing professional's company regarding the supplier's work or product, the insurer will most likely accept the claim more quickly.

The insurance clause will also quite often contain language indicating a waiver of subrogation in favor of the purchasing professional. Subrogation means that the supplier's insurance company pursues reimbursement from the purchasing professional's insurance company for claims they paid that were caused by the actions of someone in the purchasing professional's company. *Waiver* of subrogation in favor of the purchasing professional then prevents the supplier's insurer from pursuing reimbursement from the purchasing professional's insurer for such claims.

On top of all of this, we have the various monetary levels of insurance required for each category, which cannot be prescribed in this book, because it is entirely dependent on a myriad of factors related to the companies involved, the nature of the work being done, and the legal and risk management exposures that may be prevalent during the course of business between the parties.

Supplier's desired position: The supplier will want to support the contract with existing types and levels of insurance that they currently have. If they need to purchase a new type of insurance, or increase their coverage levels on existing insurance, they will want to pass through the costs to the purchasing professional, who from their perspective is the sole and exclusive reason for the corresponding rate increases.

They will also want to maintain and not waive subrogation rights. They should not have any issue with providing a copy of the certificate of insurance that also shows the purchasing professional's company as an additional insured.

Your desired position: The purchasing professional should as an opening position request exactly what the standard contract stipulates for the insurance clause. However, care should be

161

taken to use the correct contract form. For instance, if a beverage delivery service is being contracted with, there will be not only goods provided, but also services, in the form of delivery – which means suppliers being on the purchasing professional's company property. That means a goods and services long form template should be used. Using a goods long form template may result in the accidental omission of critical insurance provisions.

Should the supplier come back and state that they will incur additional costs to fulfill these requirements, the purchasing professional should refrain from making a hard stand and forcing this level of insurance. A risk assessment first needs to be done to determine what the risks are, and what the benefits are of having the supplier gain this additional type and/or level of insurance. Most big companies have a risk management department, and they should be consulted in this decision, especially where any exceptions are concerned. In some cases, such as with an independent consultant who cannot afford, say a $1 million commercial liability policy, it may not make business sense to force such costs onto them, regardless of whether those costs are passed through to the purchasing professional or not. There is no right answer, and this must be a case by case assessment.

N.   Background check

Purpose of the clause: This clause is in place to ensure that supplier personnel that are either in a position of trust (e.g. handling sensitive information) or that may have access to the purchasing professional's facilities, assets, or employees have passed a criminal background check. The clause will also typically stipulate that no such charges shall be pending either, and that these background checks must be passed before any given supplier employee can be assigned work in support of the contract with the purchasing professional.

The typical sort of things that are looked at pertain to onsite supplier employees includes social security tracing, county level criminal search in all counties as found by the trace, and a national sex offender search. A drug test may also be given to said employees. There are other, less common searches that are done in certain circumstances, as shown below:

Credential / Education Verification

Employee Credit Report

Employment History Verification

FDA Debarment

Federal Criminal

Global Sanctions and Enforcement Check

Global Watch Alert (Prohibited Parties)

Healthcare Sanctions Check

Medical License Verification

Military Search

Motor Vehicle Report

National Criminal Database

Office of Inspector General

Professional License Verification

Professional Reference Check

State Sexual Offender Search

Statewide Criminal

Worker's Compensation Verification

Supplier's desired position: The supplier's objectives are the same as the purchasing professional's in this case; both parties want employees that pass the background test supporting the purchasing professional. The supplier's primary concerns may be the necessity of some of the types of searches and also cost. In general, most large scale service suppliers are well prepared for such requests and have already engaged in such searches prior to having ever hired the individual into their company.

Your desired position: To align with the legal department and ensure that all appropriate background checks are included in the contract where sensitive information is involved or the supplier will have access to the purchasing professional's company assets or employees. No negotiations should happen with regards to these requirements once established, other than who pays for the individual searches. Typically this is the supplier's responsibility, unless the search requested is something non-industry standard that is uniquely being requested by the purchasing professional, in which case the purchasing professional should pay for such tests.

O.   Limitation of liability

Purpose of the clause: Seeing this clause in a purchasing contract is usually not a good thing for a purchasing professional. In fact, in nearly all cases, this clause should not be in place at all in any standard purchasing contracts. However, if one were to look at the contracts on the sales side of the same organization, this clause would be present. Why is that the case?

The reason is that the standard purchasing contract implicitly has open ended damage clauses, meaning that there are no caps or limits on the amount of damages that can be incurred by either party in the course of contract dealings. For the purchasing professional, this is a great thing. For the sales professional, this means liability and risk exposure. It means their lawyers will raise concerns and will insist that limitations on such liability must be introduced.

Recall we covered direct, consequential, and liquidated damages in previous sections. Liquidated Direct and consequential damages are typically what suppliers want to limit. Direct damages are limited in time and space to the event that caused the damages. Consequential damages are those expenses that follow as a result of the event. The scary one for suppliers is usually consequential damages. The reason for that is usually the fear of being responsible for lost profits as a result of the event that caused the damages.

The safest thing from a supplier's perspective is to limit this exposure. Recall the example we referenced earlier with the Space Shuttle Challenger. Direct damages from a simple o-ring failure could cost in the billions. Now assume that an o-ring failed in a piece of manufacturing equipment. The direct damages from a failure might be minimal – possibly only the cost of the equipment, assuming no other immediate damage. However, the consequential damages from lost profits due to downtime in manufacturing could potentially put a supplier out of business. Even liquidated damages could pose a threat, in particular if such damages can aggregate over time, such as with daily liquidated damage charges for late delivery.

Given the above, suppliers want to insert a clause that limits liability on these damages. They can specify a particular type of damage only being limited in liability, or they can state that all damages shall be limited in liability. The next question is how they determine what the liability limit will be. Invariably, the default option that suppliers propose and pursue is to limit the value of damages (usually all damages) to the value of the contract. This way, suppliers can be sure that the most that they can lose through damages claims will not exceed the revenues received through the course of contract dealings, and no further damages shall be incurred. When negotiating away from this position, suppliers typically still want to characterize the limit in such terms, e.g. one and a half times the value of the contract, two times the value of the contract, etc. They may agree to have direct damages open ended, but consequential damages capped at a certain level. It all depends on the circumstances – the supplier, the product or service, and where it is going and how it will be used.

Supplier's desired position: As stated earlier, suppliers will invariably want to introduce a limitation of liability clause into your contracts, and your contracts should otherwise have no reference to such clauses when first sending the contract to said suppliers. This may be one of the most common areas that suppliers want to see modification to the purchasing professional's contract, and for good reason – financial exposure reasons that we have already reviewed above. The supplier's opening position will most likely be that there is a limitation of liability on all damages, capped to the value of the contract. Their second position may be that all damages are capped to two times the value of the contract. In order for the supplier to agree to have no caps whatsoever, they have to really want the business, and they have to believe that the exposure is either minimal or worth the risk.

Your desired position: The ideal position here is to stay completely silent on the issue of limitation of liability in the contract. The reader must note that this is one of those examples where it is not just what is in the contract that is important, but also what is not in the contract that is important. In staying silent, the contract will have no language regarding damage limitations, and therefore there none.

There are cases where it may make sense to agree to a limitation of liability, and this is strictly a business decision. It must be emphasized that this is not a legal decision, although the legal department may take great interest in the final outcome. It is a business decision because, ultimately, the division that is requesting these products or services from this supplier will likely be the divisional profit and loss that has to absorb the financial impacts of any direct or consequential damages that are left uncovered as a result of this agreement.

Therefore, if a supplier absolutely refuses to sign a contract absent a limitation of liability clause, two things need to happen. The first is that there needs to be an immediate assessment done to see if this is the supplier that must be used. Are there other options? How badly do we need to work with this specific supplier? What is the next best alternative? The supplier needs to know that their lack of willingness to agree to the exclusion of a limitation of liability clause may cost them the business. If the answer to these questions is that this supplier must be used, then we go to the second course of action, which is seeking very high levels of approval with the customer's division for this limitation of liability.

Once again, the reason is that this senior manager (preferably a VP level) is the one who will be ultimately responsible for such damages, and so this person must buy off on the contract. With this express approval (meaning, in writing – email is usually fine), the purchasing person can then demonstrate to the legal department that the corresponding business unit has understood and accepted the financial risk and exposure, and based on that approval, receive legal department approval on the contract.

This process should be the exception and not the norm. The vast majority of the time, the purchasing professional should be able to negotiate and execute to contracts with no limitation of liability language incorporated, or with a very broad level of coverage, such as five times the value of the contract.

P.   Indemnification

Purpose of the clause: The word "indemnify" means to hold harmless, specifically from third party claims. Whenever this clause is in a contract, this is exactly what is being sought. However, the exact context must be understood. Specifically, it must be understood who is indemnifying whom, and for what reasons and under what conditions. Used properly and with good business intent, the purpose of the indemnification clause is to ensure that each party is held responsible for their own actions and inactions – for areas in their direct control.

Let us take the example of a company that has designed a chip, and wants to outsource manufacturing of this design to a third party. The manufacturing supplier will rightfully have some intellectual property (hereafter, IP) concerns. For instance, let us say that this product design is found to have infringed on some other company's patent. The responsible party should be the designers of this chip, not the manufacturers. The manufacturer is simply doing what they have been told – build a chip to this exact specification. Therefore, if the manufacturer gets sued by the company whose IP has been infringed, they would want to be held harmless, or indemnified.

Now let us change this example slightly. Let us say that the purchasing organization did not design this chip. Let us say instead that the manufacturing company designed it, and then the purchasing organization that bought these chips and embedded in their products for sale got sued for IP infringement. In such case, the purchasing organization would want to be indemnified for IP infringement. Once again, this makes sense, because it is the manufacturer that designed this product, not the purchasing organization. The purchasing organization is only the messenger.

In this modified circumstance above, the purchasing organization would instead be indemnified, and there should be no discussion or negotiation about it. The goal is not to gain an unfair advantage or to force the other party to be responsible for something outside of their scope of control. The goal is for each party to be responsible for that which is within their control.

Supplier's desired position: The supplier, if ethical, will only seek indemnification for areas where they should not rightly be held financially and legally responsible. If unethical, they may try to shift liability for areas within their immediate control to the purchasing professional.

<u>Your desired position</u>: The purchasing professional should

have one objective and one objective only when dealing with

this clause, and that is ensuring that each party is accountable

for their own decisions, actions, and inactions. The following

is a list of scenarios along with notation of which party should

be indemnified in the contract in each situation:

Circumstance	Party That Should Be Indemnified	
	Supplier	**Purchasing**
Purchasing develops design and has supplier build. IP infringement risk arises.	X	
Supplier develops design and sells to supplier to embed in their products. IP infringement risk arises		X
Construction supplier employee drills a hole through hand in the course of routine work as defined by supplier's management.		X
Supplier managed customer data center is damaged because customer smoked a cigarette in the data center room, causing the overhead sprinklers to turn on and damage all the equipment	X	
Supplier is driving in purchasing's parking lot, isn't paying attention, and hits and kills somebody.		X
Janitorial company spills chemical in the hallway, does not take proper precautions, and employee slips and hurts themselves on the liquid.		X
Janitorial company uses purchasing professional specified chemicals, which result in noxious fumes and allergic reactions by many employees.	X	
Rental car company under contract to purchasing professional issues a car to an employee with faulty brakes, resulting in a tragic car accident.		X

Q.   Force majeure/contingencies

Purpose of the clause: "Force majeure" is French for "major

force". It is also sometimes called contingencies. The purpose

of this clause is to allow the party to which is applies to be

relieved of their contractual responsibilities, and usually any

corresponding damages that may arise as a result, if certain

unpredictable events outside of their control incapacitate that

party in some way.

Without intent to invoke religious ideology, these occurrences

are typically and often referred to as "acts of God" in

purchasing and supplier contract templates. Incidents that may

occur that typically fall under this umbrella include such

incidents as war, tornado, hurricane, city flood (as opposed to

building flood), tsunami, earthquake, and other natural or

uncontrollable disasters. It is therefore understood that if a

hurricane ruins a supplier manufacturing facility, they should not be held liable if they are unable to make on time delivery as a result.

A couple of problems arise with this clause however, and we will cover those in the two sections that follow.

Supplier's desired position: The supplier will often attempt to expand this clause from "acts of God" to include anything and everything that will allow them to escape responsibility for things that are or should be in their control. For example, suppliers will typically try to insert the following into the force majeure/contingencies clause:

- Late deliveries by their suppliers
- Utilities disruption
- Employee strike
- Management strike
- Manufacturing downtime or disruption
- Etc.

<u>Your desired position</u>: By attempting to insert the types of items above in the force majeure/contingencies clause, the supplier is in reality only checking to see if the purchasing professional is paying attention. Suppliers know full well that these criteria, while legally enforceable in this clause if added, have no business being there and are completely inconsistent with the original spirit and intent of the clause. There is absolutely no reason why the purchasing professional should agree to any such additions to this standard clause language, and suppliers will invariably agree to return to the original language with little to no complaint. It may say something about the suppliers that try to create such contract loopholes – what else are they to do to absolve themselves of responsibility for contract performance? The purchasing professional should be vigilant.

R.   Dispute resolution: arbitration, mediation, litigation

<u>Purpose of the clause</u>: There will always be disputes between the purchasing professionals firm and suppliers. This is normal, and can even be healthy, as disputes can also result in innovation in problem solving. However, what both parties don't want, or at least the purchasing professional shouldn't want, is that disputes immediately result in litigation. There should be a dispute path that is followed, something that is an alternative to litigation. In fact, this path is often called alternative dispute resolution (ADR) for this reason.

This dispute resolution path, in its most complete form, starts with management discussions and negotiations, which if unsuccessful is followed by mediation, which if unsuccessful is followed by arbitration, which if unsuccessful is followed by litigation.

The overwhelming desire, however, should be to start with negotiations. Moving from here to mediation and arbitration allows the parties to be more in control of the process and also to avoid the uncertainty, costs, and time allocation associated with the courtroom.

Mediation is an attractive alternative to litigation. Mediators are individuals trained in negotiations, who then bring both parties together and attempt to work out a settlement or agreement between the two. Mediation is typically non-binding.

Arbitration is a less bureaucratic version of a legal hearing, as compared to a courtroom trial. Some differences involved include limited discovery and simplified rules of evidence. The arbitration is headed and decided by an arbitral panel, and their decisions are typically binding and generally enforceable under both state and federal law.

ADR can follow any format at all however. It can be defined as going straight from negotiation to mediation to litigation, bypassing mediation altogether, for instance. Or it can go straight from negotiation to binding arbitration. There can also be key stipulations put in place, such as that the arbitrators must have an electrical engineering degree, if the case at hand is highly technical and involves proprietary engineering negotiations. All of this can be determined by both parties in advance. After the parties are already in dispute is a bad time to try to determine how disputes should be resolved.

Supplier's desired position: When the contract is being formed, the supplier will have every intention to want to avoid litigation. At that point, there are no disputes, and there are no feelings of ill-will. Suppliers will generally agree to a contract clause that defines an ADR process whereby disputes first are dealt by negotiation between the parties. Most suppliers are also open to mediation as the next step, because mediation is typically focused on trying to achieve harmony between the parties, and there is nothing to lose if the outcome is not to either party's liking because it is usually non-binding.

After mediation is where it becomes a little bit tricky. Some companies are wary of arbitration, for different reasons. They may prefer to avoid it altogether, and to make it difficult for the case to go to a court of law, because of all the time and costs involved. This may be a motivational tool to try and resolve the dispute at the lowest level possible, which is the goal of ADR. Therefore, it cannot be anticipated what the supplier expected position will be beyond negotiation and mediation. Arbitration and litigation are both touchy subjects that make both parties nervous. The supplier will likely take direction from their internal legal department, whose point of view will be entirely dependent on the circumstances of this contract, that company's school of thought on ADR, and their past experiences with ADR.

Your desired position: Purchasing should have only one goal, as should the supplier, and that is to resolve issues and disputes at the lowest possible level. This means starting with negotiations. This can be stipulated in the contract in an ADR clause – something that is not always found in standard purchasing contract templates. After that, as with the supplier's stance, the purchasing professional's stance will rely entirely on the circumstance, the criticality of the purchase, the company's standard practice, and the legal department's perspective on such matters. There is no right or wrong answer, other than the strong guidance to try to resolve issues at the lowest level possible, with the goal of resolving any and all disputes in the negotiation stage wherever and whenever possible.

S.   Entire Agreement

Purpose of the clause: This clause is intended to convey that the entire agreement between the parties is captured in the four corners of the contract between the parties, and supersedes any other agreements that take place before, during, or after the contract negotiations, in whatever format they may take place, with the exception of amendments and addendums that are signed by authorized representatives of both parties. This means that both parties must be very vigilant in capturing every aspect of the agreement within the four corners of the contract that is signed between the parties. Separate agreements made in discussions, over mail, in separate documents, etc all are made contractually non-binding by this clause. The only way then to modify the contract is by amendment or addendum.

As such, this contract clause can be a blessing to both parties. It is a blessing in that side agreements and discussions are not a part of the agreement – the contract is all that matters. This is particularly valuable for the purchasing professional from the perspective that customer agreements with the supplier do not become a binding part of the contract. The courts still reserve the right to rule differently however.

Having said the above, this clause can also be a curse, for the same reasons that it is a blessing: every change requires a formal process of amendments and/or addendums, which are time consuming, require signatures, etc. Additionally, side agreements and commitments are not technically binding as a part of the contract between the parties. Once again, the courts reserve the right to rule differently, but this should not be something either party relies upon.

Supplier's desired position: The supplier should be 100% on board with this clause. In theory, it is in both parties best interest to have all aspects of the agreement captured in the contract. In practice, this may present some administrative difficulties, but this is generally not a consideration at the time of contract review and signature.

Your desired position: Purchasing should also want this clause, because it encourages the desirable behavior of having a contract that comprehensively documents the agreement between the parties. It also discourages the supplier from striking side agreements with internal customers. Finally, in the event of a dispute that results in litigation, it encourages (but does not require) the courts to look exclusively at the contract to determine the agreement between the parties, rather than course of past conduct, side agreements, or standard practices in either party's industry.

T.   Survival Clauses

Purpose of the clause: This is a very valuable provision in a contract that ensures that certain clauses do not expire along with the rest of the contract. For instance, if two companies are sharing confidential technology information, the fact that the contract between them expires does not suddenly make the information no longer confidential. The information should still be kept confidential (unless the companies wish or decide otherwise), even if the parties decide to allow the contract between them to lapse, for whatever reason. There are a number of predictable scenarios where this clause is valuable. These are usually tied to such clauses as confidential information, intellectual property, indemnification, and limitation of liability.

With intellectual property, there may be issues or agreements that need to stay in place in perpetuity. As it pertains to indemnification and limitation of liability, there may be incidents or damages that take place after the expiration of the agreement that still need ongoing coverage. For instance, if an intellectual property infringement lawsuit is filed against the purchasing professional's firm by a third party for which the supplier should be responsible, the expiration of the agreement is not reason for the purchasing professional's firm not to still be indemnified.

The survival clause is a separate clause that then references all the other clauses in the contract that shall survive the expiration of the agreement. The other clauses referenced do not need to be in sequential order, and can in fact be completely spread out in the contract – their order and distribution is of no legal relevance.

Supplier's desired position: There are typically no issues raised by the supplier on survival clauses, assuming it is proposed for areas that make business sense for both parties involved.

Your desired position: The purchasing professional should seek to not accept modification to any of the standard clauses

U.   Termination (cause, convenience)

Purpose of the clause: There are two types of termination clauses: termination for convenience and termination for cause (sometimes also called termination for default). Another important concept is whether these clauses are unilateral or

190

bilateral, meaning if such termination rights are granted to only one party or to both parties. We will explore all angles.

Termination for convenience is exactly what it says: the contract can be terminated at any time, for any reason – in fact, no reason needs to be given. However, there is also language that is normally included in this clause that indicates that any work in process by the other party (usually the supplier) will be fairly compensated for by the terminating party (usually the purchasing professional) at the time of termination.

For instance, if a supplier is manufacturing 100 widgets for the purchasing professional and they receive a termination for convenience notice. Assume that this product has a five part manufacturing process and the termination notice came in after these 100 widgets went through part three of the manufacturing process. The purchasing professional must pay for work in process manufacturing costs incurred, however, this is not as simple as paying for 60% (3/5 = .6 = 60%) of the product cost to the supplier, as the costs may and likely are spread out in a disproportionate fashion across the five steps. Therefore, there must be an algorithm that is agreed upon between the two parties to fairly compensate for costs reasonably incurred as a consequence of the termination.

The example above is in fact a perfect scenario for the need to introduce a liquidated damages clause in a contract. This clause may state for instance that if the contract (or an order) is cancelled after step one of the manufacturing process, 11% of the product price is due. After step two, 27%. After step three, 43%. After step four, 77%. After step five, 100% of the product price is due, because the product was already completed upon receipt of termination notice. It is better to negotiate such scenarios up front rather than when a termination must be processed.

With termination for cause, there must be specific triggers that allow the party with such rights to cancel with the other. For instance, the supplier may be given contract rights to terminate for cause in the event of continued lack of payment on the part of the purchasing professional's firm (usually the only scenario whereby a supplier can exercise termination for cause). To be clear, it is not advocated for the purchasing professional to agree to the supplier having such contractual rights, this is just an example of where they might have such right. The purchasing professional may be given termination for cause rights in the event of delayed delivery, product quality issues, supplier financial default, material breach of contract, fraud, and other such areas that give reasonable cause for the purchasing professional to immediately terminate the agreement. Under termination for cause clauses, typically work in process costs by the supplier are not reimbursed, because it was the supplier's material failure to perform that resulted in the termination. Therefore, when the purchasing professional is faced with an opportunity to either terminate for convenience or for cause, the latter is preferable from a cost management perspective.

Supplier's desired position: The supplier will likely either want both parties to have termination for convenience rights or for neither to have them. Many suppliers will not sign a contract where the customer company has termination for convenience rights, and will attempt to negotiate for bilateral termination for cause rights. This will give the purchasing professional rights to cancel the contract only if certain material triggers are met, and will give the supplier the right to cancel the contract if their defined triggers are met (which again is usually limited to prolonged non-payment by the purchasing professional, despite repeated requests and warnings by the supplier). As a backup, most suppliers will seek to have a unilateral termination for cause clause in the purchasing professional's favor, and no termination for convenience clause whatsoever.

<u>Your desired position</u>: The purchasing professional should strive to have a unilateral termination for convenience clause in their favor (this may or may not already be in the purchasing professional's standard contract templates) as well as a unilateral termination for convenience clause in their favor.

There is far too much risk involved with allowing suppliers to have termination for convenience rights. Even the mundane, such as office products providers, could cause business disruption if they suddenly decide to terminate for no reason. On the more serious front, if a direct materials supplier decides to suddenly terminate without reason, it could be devastating to the business. Nearly every purchase category in the company would have to be multi-sourced in anticipation of such, which is completely unreasonable and unacceptable. Therefore, suppliers should never have termination for convenience rights.

As a backup position, the purchasing professional may agree to allow the supplier to have termination for cause rights only.

This would have to be under very particular circumstances where the purchasing professional's firm failed to render payment that was contractually due, and despite repeated notices and demands for payment, failed to do so for a period for a period of six months or longer. Simply making a late payment cannot and must not be the low hurdle that must be met for the supplier to exercise termination for cause rights. The hurdle must be very high and very difficult to reach for the supplier, giving the purchasing professional ample time to intervene and solve problems that are preventing contractually due payments to the supplier.

Chapter V: Post Contract Management

Post contract management comprises all activities that happen after the contract is signed.   Unfortunately, for too many purchasing professionals, that means filing the copy in a cabinet and quickly moving onto the next one.   The thought process here is that after contract signature, the heavy lifting is done and it's time to claim victory. Nothing could be further from the truth.

There are several aspects of post contract management that need to be looked at.   These are as follows:

1. Contract storage, confidentiality, and best practices sharing

2. Contract terms compliance

3. Breach management

4. Contract expenditure compliance

5. Contract retirement and disposition

We will start with contract storage. Let's get the most important point out of the way: the worst place a purchasing professional can store a contract is in a file cabinet. The second worse place is on a personal computer hard drive. The reason is that a contract is a company asset that must be managed, accessed, and protected. It is no more acceptable for a purchasing professional to keep contracts in a file cabinet or on a pc than it is for the IRS to have tax returns spread out in various file cabinets and employee computers as their primary system of storage. Virtually every seasoned purchasing professional I've met with has experienced the frustration of starting an exciting new purchasing position, only to find an empty file cabinet. The only thing worse than that is the humiliation of having to ask suppliers for a copy of your own contract with them. This shouldn't be happening to anyone in our profession.

The next level of evolution in contract storage is the shared drive concept, whereby everyone with access rights can find the necessary contracts. This is great in concept, but in reality is rarely successful. The reason is that shared drives typically lack any sort of management structure or controls to keep the content organized properly, updated, managed for change control, and updated with the latest information. As a consequence, shared drives tend to become glorified dumping grounds over time, whatever the original purpose. Posting the information is not the challenge – administrating it properly is.

What is most ideal is an online, secure access intranet or software application that allows for contract storage and access. I will not make recommendations for particular solutions, but I will say that these sorts of solutions can be purchased or developed in house. These systems must have a number of capabilities. These include:

- Being able to give bullet-proof secure access rights to individuals with a need to know, while not allowing anyone outside that list access.

- Having a structured database capability such that contracts can be searched for by owner, supplier, commodity, signature date, expiration date, dollar amount assigned to the contract, and any other categories that are important to the purchasing professional.

- Having access to both the signed and working copy of the document (usually in Microsoft Word). This is important because the signed copy is the official legal version and the working copy of the document can be used to copy and paste sections for use in other contracts (we will discuss this later).

- Being able to track contract approvals, such as by purchasing management and by legal. This is important for reasons related to verification of internal controls, both by purchasing and by internal audit.

- Being able to assign a unique contract number, for overall contract tracking purposes.

- Being able to recognize duplicate entries or potential duplicate entries. For instance, if a contract is being uploaded with 'IBM Inc', the system should immediately notify you that a contract exists with 'IBM Corp' and ask you if you are sure you want to add another contract with what is potentially the same supplier (most contracts are written as agreements with that entire supplier entity, in which cases the purchasing professional should add an addendum to the existing agreement instead of introducing another contract).

- Ability to recognize expired contracts and renewed contracts that replace them, while keeping both in retention per the purchasing professionals record retention policy for contracts.

- The ability to upload other documentation that is of relevance to the agreement, such as SOW/Specs, RFX, negotiation plan, etc.

- Change control capabilities to track who has access the system for which contracts on which date and time, and what specific changes were made. Ideally, these changes could then be undone at any point in time if a critical error was made. If this was not caught until several undesired revisions were made, the system would then allow you to go back enough revisions until the desired version of that document or documents is retrieved.

- The ability to assign a singular owner to each contract and to, if so desired, prevent anyone other than that owner from making changes or modifications to that contract file record.

- Ability to notify contract owners as contracts are set to expire in predefined increments, e.g. 3 months before, 2 months before, 1 month before, 1 week before, and then weekly after expiration until renewed or retired.

- Highly desirable, but hard to establish systems integration to support: ability to notify contract owners as to actual spending against contract vs negotiated expenditure volumes. This should involve preventative notices first (e.g. 50% spending against contract, 75%, 90%, 95%, 100%, etc) before the contract is overspent, following which, notices should still be auto-generated and sent (105% spending against contract, 110%, etc).

- Ability to produce reports that demonstrate aggregate assessments, such as all contracts that are expired.

- Any other areas that are of importance to your purchasing department, customer base, management team, legal team, records retention department, or internal audit. A comprehensive analysis needs to be done, because once the system is designed, there is in all likelihood little to no possibility of modifying it.

In implementing a contract database such as this, it is critical that a behavior changed is invoked with all contract owners: instead of saving contracts to their hard drive, the save them to this system. There should not be duplication of storage. Doing so will invariably lead to the same problems as before. Everything should be stored properly, and only once. To quote one of my favorite adages, there needs to be only "one version of the truth".

Another critical aspect of contract databases is that, if designed and used properly, they introduce a best practices sharing mechanism. In the "old school" model, everyone customizes their own clauses and contracts (assuming they didn't just take a standard template and use that without modification – something I don't encourage). Having an entire global organization of purchasing professionals customize and create their own contract clauses to solve the same problems is an utter and complete waste of corporate time and assets. With a solid contract database system in place, a purchasing professional in India doing a janitorial contract can go into their corporate contract database system and search for "janitorial" and then review all such other contracts in the company, both current and expired. From there, key customized clauses can be copied and pasted and used where applicable in this local contract in India.

This example above represents a dramatic shift in time savings and results improvement, and should be encouraged throughout the purchasing organization. This reuse of contract language should be far preferable to creating new language. New language is time consuming and unproven. The use of existing language is the click of a button away, and it is also proven the test of time. There could be cases where such language was in fact not well written and problems were encountered. The purchasing professional accessing the contract needs to exercise good judgment and possibly contact the original contract owner just to verify or validate any concerns.

The next thing that needs to be looked at on an ongoing basis is contract terms compliance. What this means is looking for performance *by either party* that is inconsistent with what the contract states. This is meant to be a proactive assessment, done on an ongoing basis before excursions happen. How often is up to the individual purchasing manager and the type of good or service being procured, but quarterly is a good rule of thumb – which would line up nicely with quarterly business reviews that the supplier may be engaged in with purchasing.

In doing this assessment, all performance terms should be looked at – any area where one party is to perform a particular obligation. Areas such as delivery, quality, warranty, payment (by the purchasing professionals' company), performance to schedule, customer service scores, and any other performance deliverables should all be looked at for compliance. Any breaches should be categorized as material or minor breach. The material breaches should get immediate attention, as outlined earlier in this book.

The other thing that should get looked at is if the actual agreement between the parties is still adequately captured in the four corners of the contract. Recall the "entire agreement" clause, whereby only that language which is in the contract represents the entire agreement between the parties. Therefore, if there have been side agreements or adjustments to expectations by either party that the purchasing professional wants to have enforced, it is time to update the contract with an amendment and/or addendum. A paper trail should be kept for this audit – a simple checklist and action plan is fine – for the purpose of historical tracking and to show internal audit, should they choose to audit the purchasing department.

The next area of focus is contract breach management. We already covered material and minor breach from a definitions perspective, but not yet from a management perspective. Since minor by definition is just that – minor – we will not delve into required actions needed to be addressed. Often a minor breach of contract can be resolved in a quick email or phone call, or purchasing intervention may not be needed at all.

There is yet another type of breach we need to cover as well, and that is anticipatory breach. Anticipatory breach is a circumstance where a material breach of contract has not yet taken place, but you have solid and reasonable evidence to believe that one will take place. For instance, if it is on the news that your supplier's workforce is on strike, or if your supplier's manufacturing facility is in a city in Japan that was demolished by tsunami or earthquake, or if your supplier's facility is at the center of an area where there is civil unrest, or if your supplier is sole sourced with a company that has had a public material supply line disruption, any of these and more can be reason for you to have firm belief that your supplier WILL breach the contract. They key is that the evidence not be hearsay (i.e. it comes from a reliable source), and that your interpretation of this evidence is reasonable (i.e. that you are reading the events and interpreting them in a manner that is fair and reasonable).

In the case of either material or anticipatory material breach, communication should take place in written format. Now, if timelines are urgent, a phone call may be made immediately, but written documentation is always the best policy in conjunction with this. This documentation to the supplier should be highly factual, and should have any emotions introduced whatsoever. This notification of breach must be sent from the purchasing professional and not anyone else in the company. This is an opportunity to enforce the purchasing professional's role as the undisputed single point of authority representing the purchasing organization's company. The letter, aside from the normal formalities (date, sender, receiver, etc) should have the following items contained in it:

- The recipient should be a senior level person in the company to whom the letter is being sent. The local or normal point of contact person or persons may be cc'd, but the letter should be addressed to someone who is roughly Vice President level in the company, in the appropriate division (usually customer sales).

- The letter should clearly state atop **"Notification of Material Breach of Contract"** or **"Notification of Anticipatory Material Breach of Contract"** in bold font and centered. This must be conspicuous.

- The name of both parties to the contract, the effective date of the contract, and the contract # (from the purchasing professional's system – if available or applicable) should be referenced.

- The specific contract clause that is being breached or is anticipation of being breached should be both referenced AND restated in its entirety in the letter.

- The letter must clearly spell out what the desired remedy is for breach of contract. The first choice of action is to reference existing remedies in the contract. If the contract does not have a remedy for a material breach, then the purchasing professional's expectations must be clearly laid out, and in highly specific terms: who, what, where, when, why, and how. Every single aspect of expectations for remedy of this breach must be spelled out.

- The supplier must be asked to reply with a root cause and corrective action report, indicating why this contract clause was breached (what specifically broke down that allowed this to happen), and what systemic measure they are taking to ensure it never recurs again.

- If the purchasing professional chooses to waive any of their contract rights, or to modify a defined remedy in the contract to be easier on the supplier (such as allowing a product replacement to take place in 96 hours instead of 24 hours as the contract may prescribe), then included in the letter must be language that states that "Although Buyer is making an exception and allowing for product replacement in 96 hours as a remedy in this particular case, Buyer reserves all rights provided in the contract and is not waiving contract rights to enforce 24 hour remedy for future such incidents."

- The supplier must be asked to respond in writing to all of the above by a prescribed date. If the supplier responds by phone call despite this request, then the purchasing professional should take copious notes and then send a written communication to the individual responding and to the person to whom the letter was originally addressed (if someone different) summarizing the discussion and agreement on next steps in detail. If they do not respond to this communication, then by waiver principle, it is assumed that they have waived their rights and agree.

In performing the above, it should be noted that the best purchasing contract managers are not the ones who are most adept at catching and responding to breaches of contract, but rather those who have written the contract and selected and managed the supplier in such a way as to prevent them from ever happening in the first place.

Another important area of focus, not from a legal perspective, but from a negotiation perspective, is a contract expenditure compliance system. Contracts are negotiated with a particular value in mind. This is almost always the case. The purchasing professional has a target expenditure level against which they are negotiating their volume discount schedule. If the purchasing professional negotiates a contract with $500,000 expenditures in mind over a given period, they will receive commensurate levels of discount (which will vary based on circumstances and the skill of the purchasing professional). However, if $1,000,000 is instead spent during this period without the purchasing professional's knowledge, then money has been left on the table. This is one of the biggest tragedies in purchasing – easy money left on the table.

The ideal is that the contract database tracks this information and reports it before such expenditure overruns happen. This is a rare feature in a contract database and if this capability cannot be found in any corporate system, then a manual system needs to be developed and regular auditing needs to happen.

There will be instances where the expenditure overrun has already happened by the time purchasing does the audit. Do not despair! Money should never be left on the table – ever. The purchasing professional should go back to the supplier and negotiate new pricing based on this increased level of spending and negotiate for this new pricing to be retroactive to the point at which the contract value was exceeded – which may be months earlier. This is perfectly acceptable.

One thing the purchasing professional can do when writing contracts that are subject to such cost overruns is to include a clause such as the following in the contract, in order to facilitate such retroactive pricing negotiations at a later date (remember: you must take such language in front of your management and legal chain before using – this is not legal advice):

"Should the expenditures against this contract for the stated period exceed the agreed upon contract value of \$_____, Supplier shall immediately notify Buyer, and Buyer reserves the right to renegotiate the contract accordingly. Should the contract be overspent in this capacity, Supplier agrees that any new and lower pricing arrangements shall be retroactive to any such expenditures by which the contract was overspent, and shall provide prompt reimbursement or credit to Buyer."

One reason which such overspends happen is that the supplier is contacted by a different customer internally and that customer initiates new business and new expenditures, unbeknownst to the purchasing professional. This can be similarly dealt with by having a custom clause such as the following embedded in the contract during negotiations, aiding in preventing such activities:

"Should supplier be contacted by any individual within buyer's company with intent to contract with supplier or purchase goods or services outside of the immediate scope of this agreement, Supplier shall immediately contact Buyer and advise him/her of this request and shall not proceed until such time that buyer provides express approval.   In such cases, Buyer reserves the right to renegotiate the contract to reflect this increased business."

The last thing that needs to be looked at is contract retirement and dispositioning. Retirement takes place when business with the supplier is no longer intended or needed, and therefore the contract is either terminated, allowed to expire, or not renewed. Dispositioning entails actually taking the contract out of the purchasing department's system, whatever that system may be (file cabinet, shared drive, online contract database, etc).   Just because a contract is retired does not mean it's not needed. Sometimes delivery happens after a contract is retired, or a warranty issue arises post-retirement, or a contract breach of another sort (such as patent infringement) takes place later.

On top of these reasons, there are reasons related to audit and compliance that necessitate these contracts be kept on file for some period. This is usually determined by senior purchasing leadership, the legal department, and the records retention department. The purchasing professional should not decide on their own how long to keep retired contracts on file. Ultimately, there is no right answer, but five years seems to be around where the industry tries to keep itself. Where there are IP considerations, some contracts may be kept indefinitely.

If the contract is written correctly up front – customized to identify performance criteria and written such that excursions are largely prevented and in such a way to enable supplier continuous quality improvement, post contract management is a routine process that takes little time.

If a contract is comprised of attaching a supplier quotation to a standard boilerplate contract, the purchasing professional will spend inordinately more time dealing with issues that were never addressed in the contract. Even worse, the supplier will now offer resistance and will want more money to meet the purchasing professional's undocumented expectations. This is the more frequent scenario, and it doesn't need to be this way. Follow the direction in this book to customize contracts up front and to write performance oriented contracts.

Chapter VI: Final Thoughts

In twenty years and counting of teaching, consulting, and coaching on purchasing and supply chain concepts across every industry and every geography, I have been continuously been both disheartened and disappointed to find that purchasing professionals the world over lack the necessary contract skills to achieve world class purchasing results, and also are unaware of this missing piece in their arsenal.

Somehow they look for every opportunity to have the legal department own the contracts, and view contracts and legal department engagement as necessary evil in the negotiation process. Those who I am able to spend time with are transformed and suddenly realize that the contract is not a requirement, it is a critical enabler of results, a saver of time, anti-lock brakes that prevent accidents instead of an airbag that protects after an accident. Contracts are a vehicle to capture your unique requirements and make sure they are met in a way that leaves you hours of free time on your schedule and with much better results. Putting time into your contracts means you will be buying results instead of goods and services. It means you will have time to work on strategy while your peers scramble to put out fires.

Unfortunately, what I see is an industry of purchasing professionals that are largely fire fighters. What I want to see is a set of people who write contracts in such a way to not allow these fires to start, and to then watch as their results grow, their careers grow, and their income grows.

It's really not that hard. You have a decision to make though. Do you want to pay now, or pay later, only ten times as much or more when paying later? Make the shift now to being a proactive purchasing professional that embraces contracts, understands contracts, writes them to buy results, and writes them to generate results, in a hands-off fashion.

Purchasing is supposed to be a lucrative and fulfilling profession. Not everyone in this profession experiences that though. The shifts that I am asking you to take in this book form the foundation for putting you on that track. Now go off and do something wonderful with your new found knowledge!

About the Author

Omid Ghamami has 18 years' experience with Intel Corp, holding responsibility for ~ $1 Billion in annual expenditures as a senior purchasing executive, and also having managed their global purchasing operations.

He has broad experience in negotiations, total cost analysis, supply chain management, purchasing contract law, purchasing operations, purchasing policies and procedures, controls & risk management, selection & deployment of purchasing systems/tools, M & A integration, and purchasing strategy mapping/execution.

He was responsible for the end to end negotiation planning, execution, and training processes for the entire $2.2B global procurement organization. His transformational results for the company and the global purchasing organization resulted in him being named THE Godfather of Negotiation Planning.

Omid is President & Chief Consultant at Purchasing Advantage, a purchasing seminar and training solutions provider. Since 1995, he has taught thousands of hours of acclaimed courses, workshops, & seminars in 14 different countries on topics related to the entire spectrum of purchasing, supply chain management, purchasing contract law, negotiations, and supplier management. In this capacity, he provides world class consulting, corporate training, public seminars, personal coaching, group coaching, purchasing organization transformation support, conference seminar & guest speakership, to individuals and companies all over the world.

Omid's competitive edge is not only deep and rich purchasing knowledge, but also a transformational teaching style that focuses on revamping how purchasing is done from the bottom up, such that purchasing organizations and professionals slash the amount of time they spend on non-value added activities by 75% or more, and shift focus to more strategic and value added activities that catapult individual and departmental results. All solutions are broken down to specific steps, activities, and templates, such that all barriers to achieving purchasing excellence are eliminated.

Omid holds a Bachelor's degree in Business Administration with a concentration in Finance and a minor in Economics from California State University, Sacramento, as well as an MBA from the University of California, Riverside (Class President).

Omid is also an esteemed Adjunct Professor of Purchasing in the Los Rios Community College District, where he has pioneered the development of an innovative purchasing curriculum that is the first of its kind in the California community college system and has received many accolades.